Narrative Imagination and Everyday Life

Explorations in Narrative Psychology

Mark Freeman
Series Editor

Books in the Series

Speaking of Violence
Sara Cobb

Narrative Imagination and Everyday Life
Molly Andrews

NARRATIVE IMAGINATION AND EVERYDAY LIFE

Molly Andrews

OXFORD
UNIVERSITY PRESS

OXFORD
UNIVERSITY PRESS

Oxford University Press is a department of the University of Oxford.
It furthers the University's objective of excellence in research, scholarship,
and education by publishing worldwide.

Oxford   New York
Auckland   Cape Town   Dar es Salaam   Hong Kong   Karachi
Kuala Lumpur   Madrid   Melbourne   Mexico City   Nairobi
New Delhi   Shanghai   Taipei   Toronto

With offices in
Argentina   Austria   Brazil   Chile   Czech Republic   France   Greece
Guatemala   Hungary   Italy   Japan   Poland   Portugal   Singapore
South Korea   Switzerland   Thailand   Turkey   Ukraine   Vietnam

Oxford is a registered trademark of Oxford University Press
in the UK and certain other countries.

Published in the United States of America by
Oxford University Press
198 Madison Avenue, New York, NY 10016

Library of Congress Cataloging-in-Publication Data
Andrews, Molly.
Narrative imagination and everyday life / Molly Andrews.
   pages cm
Includes bibliographical references and index.
ISBN 978–0–19–981239–4
1. Imagination.   2. Narration (Rhetoric)—Psychological aspects.   I. Title.
BF408.A54 2013
153.3—dc23
2013017561

9 8 7 6 5 4 3 2 1
Printed in the United States of America
on acid-free paper

Dedicated in loving memory
Siyanda Ndlovu
(1982 – 2010)

CONTENTS

ACKNOWLEDGEMENTS

I am indebted to many people for making this book possible. Indeed, the topic is so over-arching, that really I should begin in my early years and work my way forward, identifying those individuals who have helped me to see the world from a slightly different angle. But that would be too much. Rather I will limit myself here to the most immediate influences which have contributed to the book's creation.

I have been lucky to have had ongoing conversations through the years with some very smart and generous people: Jens Brockmeier, Wolfgang Edelstein, Mark Freeman, Ruthellen Josselson, Ann Phoenix, Cathy Riessman, Birgit Schmitt, Nira Yuval-Davis, Shirin Rai and Jeremy Roche, thank you.

The Centre for Narrative Research provides a very special place for scholarship and community, which includes not only our members near and far, but also our exceptional post-graduate students. Corinne Squire, Maria Tamboukou, and Cigdem Esin, thank you for keeping life at CNR rolling, and to all of our students and visitors who help to make it such a vibrant place. I would not have been able to write the book had I not been granted a sabbatical from the University of East London.

The book owes its existence firstly to Mark Freeman, who nurtured the idea from the beginning and who provided very thoughtful and sometimes challenging feedback on the original draft. Abby Gross and Suzanne Walker at Oxford University Press have been most supportive and patient, helping to guide the project to its fruition.

Thank you to my sister, Julia Andrews, Director of the Fine Arts Program at the National Geographic Society, who helped me to find an image from their archives to use as the cover for this book.

My parents Joan and Peter Andrews read the first complete draft of the book, and gave me their characteristic blend of support and candid feedback.

And last but always first, thank you Ted, Charlotte and Peter who make everyday life fertile ground for the imagination.

Narrative Imagination and Everyday Life

CHAPTER 1

Introduction: Trafficking In Human Possibilities

Narrative and imagination are integrally tied to one another; that they are so is immediately clear to anyone who stops to think about stories—real and imagined, about the past or in a promised, or feared, future. Why and how this is so are questions that direct us to ruminate on what it means to be human.

This book takes as its starting point that narrative and imagination are combined, not only in our most elevated thoughts about the world as it might be, but also in the very minutiae of our daily lives. Although we do not often talk about the role of imagination in how we approach each day, carrying out and evading those responsibilities to which we have committed ourselves, and simply being ourselves in the world, negotiating our sometimes troubled paths between competing desires of our own and those of others, its importance cannot be overstated. It is perhaps a sign of our times that imagination, which so fascinated Aristotle and has continued to be a key concept throughout the development of Western thought, has been relatively neglected in our current age. Philosophers of the late 20th century, such as Jean Paul Sartre, devoted much time to thinking about not only the nature of imagination, but critically its function in the human psyche as well; it was through this fascination with the world as it is and its relationship to that which is not, but which may also yet be, that led Sartre to write his first well known book, *Being and Nothingness*. More recently, those inquiries into the nature of imagination which do exist are less philosophical, less contemplative, and focus more typically either on the anatomy of the brain and its critical faculties, or else on studies of fiction. During this same period, the use of a narrative lens for exploring the ways in which human beings understand and operate within complex social environments has grown exponentially. Most of this work has not dwelled upon the machinations of human imagination in the production and interpretation of narrative, although there have been some notable exceptions.[1,2] My aim here is to bring into focus the role of imagination in narrative understanding, particularly as it informs our daily lives, be it in relation to the world of politics, education, aging, or even as it relates to our perceptions of how we go about our scholarly research.

The coupling of narrative and imagination brings into focus: (1) the salience of, and dynamic nature of, the temporal; (2) a mediation between the real and the not-real; and (3) the complexity of the construction of 'the other'. Clearly, narrative and imagination are not always conjoined: many, maybe most, narratives do not concern themselves with the world of the imagination. They are, rather, limited to the world as it is 'in reality', even when that reality is always and invariably subjectively constructed. It is only when we attempt to unpack the layers of a narrative that we begin to realise the role of imagination in its construction. There are an endless number of forms that imagination can take, narrative being but one. However, when these two entities are brought into play with one another, there we encounter the balancing act which defines us as being human—living, breathing and interacting in the world even while our minds are full of memories and dreams. Brockmeier describes narrative imagination as 'the most ingenious architect of our castles real and possible'.[3] Through it, we are both anchored and transported, and it is both the tension and the synergy between these two that forms the framework of the present inquiry.

TIME TRAVELLING

Although there have been many scholars who have offered critiques of the Aristotlean conception of narrative as including a beginning, middle, and end, nonetheless, as Phillida Salmon points out, 'stories demand the consequential linking of events or ideas'. Stories are more than a mere listing of isolated occurrences. As Salmon asserts, 'the "and then" of stories includes temporal ordering, but goes beyond this in presenting some kind of humanly understandable connection'.[4] So very much is packed in to this seemingly small 'and then'—in it rests the assumption that what has gone before, and what is about to follow, belong together. They are part of a grouping, and when joined together they mean something. But exactly what is brought together and what that linkage signifies something which changes over time. Meaning is inherently unstable; even when it appears to be constant, it is nevertheless perpetually created and recreated (just as it is perpetually contested and resisted). It is here that the importance of imagination emerges. Philosopher Mary Warnock summarises the view of Sartre, that 'the imagination is that which enables us to perceive things as pointing beyond themselves, or having sense'.[5] It is imagination that lifts narrative in to another dimension and which offers it both the possibility of history and of a tomorrow.

Much has been written on the importance of expanding our conception of the temporal beyond linearity. 'Clock time', Mark Freeman tells us,

> is but one concept of time, and it does well to organise and order those features of the world characterized by linearity, by the inexorable forwardness of (certain) natural processes. But it cannot and does not do justice to those features of the human realm that go beyond linearity, that involve movement not only from past to present but from present to past, ever again.[6]

Indeed, the human psyche moves fluidly between time frames as a matter of daily course. That memory—bringing forward experiences of the past into the present—is a cornerstone of identity is clear. Without recollection, it is difficult to have a sense of who we are in the present, much less to configure a future for ourselves. We are forever revisiting our pasts, in light of changing circumstances of the present, and in so doing, our vision for the future is reconstituted.

Not only can we time travel, but we do it all the time. We must. We constantly move backwards and forwards in our mind's eye, and it is this movement which is a key stimulus behind our development. We learn from our pasts, not only as things happen, but as we reflect back on experience, in light of subsequent unfoldings. We routinely revisit moments in our lives where we now realise that, had we chosen a different path, things would have turned out very differently. We ponder the meaning of Robert Frost's 'the road not taken' in our own lives, and think about the lives we might have lived, the selves we might have become, the bad fortune that would have befallen us, had we turned at that point in the other direction. We look back on the selves we once were, selves who we are both connected to but distinct from our current selves—and this self-regard can be met with a number of different reactions, be it a fondness towards our youthful selves as we grappled to find our way, or a reticent distance from the yearnings which once occupied our hearts and minds.

Nor is our time travelling limited to our own selves. Rather, we do it about everyone, and everything. When meeting someone we know well, be it friend or foe, we regard them as someone who comes with a history. Based on our past encounters, we expect certain things from them, now in the present, and this is also the basis upon which we make plans with them, or don't, for the future. These expectations range from the mundane—someone tends to run late, or not pay their share of a bill—to the more significant—we know this person will be honest, is trustworthy, or will sell our secrets to the first person they meet—and they are themselves a form of time travel.

Even our senses of objects and space are inflected with an ongoing revision of perception and evaluation. We read a book that we have not seen since our childhood, and are surprised at the racist imagery of which we, in our youth, were oblivious. How could we have missed that message, one which so offends our current set of values? Or we revisit a place and are surprised that it is so different from the way it was in our memory. In my own life, as a young child, there was a group of 4 or 5 trees across the street from my home. These trees were taller than tall might be. Each day I would travel over to them, and climb as high as the sky. High in the trees, my siblings and I would sit and discuss life. (One day I even fell from one, and spent the next days in bed). We left that home when I was still a child, but I have seen those trees again in my adult life. Looking at them, I wondered to myself, could these small trees really be the same ones? For me they had once represented a kingdom, but now how different they appeared. But the book hasn't changed its contents, the trees have not changed their shape or height; still, in our eyes, they have become considerably altered. We come to ask ourselves what in our current lives will we later regard with a similar sense of a detached, if sometimes disappointed, curiosity? In what Ricoeur calls the 'now that...' time,[7] the encounter with our past spurs us on to imagine our future in which we are looking back on the present moment. Time traveling.

In all that I have been describing here, the role of imagination cannot be emphasized enough. Even when our memories are accurate—for instance we believe certain things happened at certain times with certain people, and we are right—the meaning which we attribute to those experiences, in other words the reason they are important to us, is highly influenced by the imaginary world we weave around them. In this sense, the word imaginary alludes to the extra bit we bring to our perception, the 'seeing beyond' referred to by Sartre earlier. It is the drive of the imagination which impels us to ask 'if only' of our past, and 'what if' of our futures. When we revisit the past, as we do when we tell stories about our lives, it is our imaginative urge which gives us the ability to contemplate a world that might have been, as well as one which might still be. It is our imagination which gives us the necessary sustenance to create visions of alternative realities, which 'differentiates human beings from all other animals'.[8]

THE REAL, THE NOT-REAL, AND THE NOT-YET-REAL

This brings us to the second point of our discussion regarding the bond between narrative and imagination. As we have just seen, narratives are not necessarily limited to life as we know it, but might derive much of their meaning when considered in relation to what Sartre calls 'the not-yet real'. Mary Warnock describes Sartre's position on this issue:

> ...man's [sic] freedom to act in the world is a function of his ability to perceive things not only as they are, but as they are not. If man could not, first, describe a present given situation both as it is and as it is not; and if he could not, secondly and consequentially, envisage a given situation as possibly being otherwise than how it is, then he would have no power to intervene in the world to change.... [Without this] he would have neither motive nor capacity for remedying his situation... the power to see things in different ways and to form images about a so far non-existent future, is identical with the power of imagination.[9]

The claim that is being made here is a very powerful one; no less is at stake than our freedom, which relies on our ability to see things not only as they are, but as they are not. In order to realise the necessary steps of transformation for traveling from A (current reality) to B (a hoped for but as yet unrealised reality) one must first create some sort of narrative emplotment, which includes characters, plot (or action), and a desired endpoint. Thus, from one's knowledge of the real, one must be able to extrapolate, to build out towards a world that is not yet real but which one day might be. In Hume's *Treatise on Human Nature* (1739), he boldly stated 'whatever the mind clearly conceives, includes the idea of possible existence, or in other words, nothing we imagine is absolutely impossible'. This maxim still holds currency; as modern philosopher Shaun Nichols comments, 'If the imagination doesn't tell us what things are possible, then it's not clear what else would'.[10] The point here is not that everything we imagine is, in fact, realisable—consider only the very rich genre of science fiction for examples of the fantastic—but, rather, that if something can be imagined, it is not 'absolutely impossible', that is, not possible in all its dimensions. Implicit here is a bridge traversing the pathway between what is known, and what can be known, between the present and possible futures.

This argument clearly relates to the first point discussed regarding temporal fluidity. The imagining of possible futures emanates from a location in the present. This discussion highlights a creative tension between temporality and possibility: just because something does not exist in the present does not mean it will not exist at a time in the future. Sartre identifies two different sorts of futures: 'the one is but the temporal ground on which my present perception develops, the other is posited for itself as *that which is not yet*'.[11] Sartre goes on to posit that a sense of ' "being-in-the-world"…is the necessary condition for the imagination'.[12] We know that the not-real might also be the not-yet-real, and that that which is real is never a static category. Movement thus connects perception with vision, extending what one sees with what one imagines. The real and the not-real are not then polar opposites but, rather, are positioned in relation to one another, linked by a thread of ongoing change and perpetual becoming.

The movement between the real and the not-real is not only temporal, but may be spatial as well. Questions of space not only direct us to where one is, but also to where one has been, and where one might go—questions

Figure 1.1:
Jean Paul Sartre was intrigued by the function of imagination in the human psyche, particularly in enabling individuals to envision the 'not-yet real'.

which are as much about physical realities as they are connected to our innermost imaginaries. Those who have been exiled from their home, and dream of returning one day, hold dear those sights, sounds, smells and tastes which for them, are indicators of that space. The spatial dimension is thus both real and imagined, and this becomes increasingly apparent when one considers for instance the power of nationalism and the role of borders.

We are often told that 'there is no view from nowhere'—regardless of how objective we may wish to be, what we see and don't see, tell and don't tell, dream and fear, remember and forget, is always and invariably linked to our particular location. Although the questioning of positioning—past, present, and future—has been a central concern of narrative scholarship (as well as a predominant theme in much feminist research over the past 25 years), this is less true in relation to work on imagination. One notable exception to this is the work of Marcel Stoetzler and Nira Yuval-Davis, who have coined the term 'situated imagination', which is presented as a 'crucial component of feminist standpoint theory' demanding that one 'account[s] for the social positioning of the social agent'.[13] What can be imagined from a particular location is integrally tied to what can be known, 'the concepts of knowing and imagining [are] complementary...the one indispensably depends on the other'.[14] Still, the relationship between the two is a complex one:

> ...situated imagination has two seemingly contradictory relationships with knowledge; on the one hand, imagination constructs its meaning while, on the other hand, it stretches and transcends them...[thus] imagination [is] both individual and collective, self- as well as other-directed, a necessary condition as well as the product of the dialogical process involved in the construction of knowledge.[15]

I will not rehearse here the epistemological arguments regarding the situatedness of knowledge, but rather will refer readers to the very dynamic feminist scholarship over the past three decades on this topic. Imagination, like knowledge, does not come out of nothingness, but is a creative synthesis which emanates from a particular location. The imagination is 'fundamental to why, whether and what we are ready to experience, perceive and know in the first place... [it] is not a straightforward faculty of the individual, but is (also, or even primarily) a social faculty'.[16]

CONSTRUCTING THE SELF AND OTHER IN NARRATIVE IMAGINATION

The third and final point regarding the vital relationship between narrative and imagination builds on the current discussion of situated knowledge.

That the 'speaking I' is always located in place, space, and time is clear, and that this fundamentally influences not only what happens in one's life but also how one makes sense of these events, is a cornerstone of much narrative scholarship. Giving accounts of ourselves is part of our everyday lives as we routinely 'order our experiences, memories, intentions, hopes, desires, fears, and concerns in an autobiographical perspective'.[17] However, the lens from which we view our lives and the world around us is one which is not only situated, but dynamic, that is to say, in a constant state of being created and recreated.

Shani Orgad's compelling study of the role of 'global imagination' in media representation provides evidence for this. The stories and images we encounter in the media and on the Internet—which are, by definition, forever changing—help to shape our individual and collective imaginations, bringing distant and faraway others, with lives that might be very unlike our own, into our living rooms. Such encounters 'feed the way we see, think of and feel about the world, about our relations with others and about our place in the world'.[18]

She lists five characteristics of imagination which impact media representation:

1. Imagination is a process of negotiation and interaction between personal and collective thinking and feeling.
2. Imagination is both factual and normative, referring to both meaningful real actions and the fantastical.
3. Imagination involves thinking and feeling, and can be messy and contradictory.
4. Imagination is dialectic.
5. Imagination is a moral force.[19]

Although Orgad's focus is on media representation, these characteristics are useful in identifying some of the ways in which imagination operates in everyday life. Exploring how we imagine others, and its relationship to how we imagine ourselves, is central to Orgad's exploration.

How and what one perceives and understands about one's own life is always connected to one's view of others. Who am I (and who are 'us') invariably invites the question of who are 'they' (or other), just as the reverse is true. This construction of self and other is ongoing, and draws equally on (situated) knowledge and imagination, reaching out not only to the future (aspirations and fears), but deeply rooted in our pasts (sometimes acknowledged, sometimes hidden). How one comes to think of oneself in relation to others and to negotiate the space between them is not only the basis of much moral philosophy, but it is something with which we are confronted every day of our lives. The challenge is practical and ethical in equal parts, and at its heart is the question of who and how we are in the world.

Mary Warnock addresses this human dilemma in the following passage:

> We are separate, certainly, each with his own point of view, but we are not irrevocably shut up in our own bodies, peering out onto the world (including the world of other people) whose real existence remains problematic...Human beings are capable of grasping and understanding the world of which they form a part. They are observers, but not observers made of wholly different stuff. Their existence is in space and time, alongside all material objects, and alongside other humans.[20]

Many other philosophers have also been occupied with this question of self and other; in the past 50 years, the work of Emmanuel Levinas has been particularly noteworthy. For Levinas, we come to know ourselves as human beings precisely through immersing ourselves in the lives of others. 'One is not called on to "love they neighbor *as* oneself'... [but rather] "love thy neighbor *is* oneself'...Care for the other trumps care for the self, is care for the self. Nothing is more significant'.[21] Levinas's work, particularly his assertion that 'the self is only possible through the recognition of the Other'[22] influenced subsequent writers, such as the Polish foreign correspondent Ryszard Kapuściński who argued 'to know ourselves we have to know Others, who act as the mirror in which we see ourselves...to understand ourselves better we have to understand Others, to compare ourselves with them, to measure ourselves against them'.[23] Referring to the work of Levinas, he writes:

> Stop, he seems to be saying to the man hurrying along in the rushing crowd. There beside you is another person. Meet him. This sort of encounter is the greatest event, the most vital experience of all. Look at the Other's face as he offers it to you. Through this face he shows you yourself...[24]

But Kapuściński's challenge, which is also our own, is how to travel the world and be open to the stories we hear, balancing a respect for common humanity with an acknowledgement of difference. If we are to avoid simply projecting onto others our own thoughts and feelings, how are we to access the world of the other? How can we be empathetic, while holding onto the important differences between the experiences of others and our own?

If there is a path through this, and we have to hope that there is, then it surely it must be through human interaction and communication, and it is based on this that an entire philosophy of dialogue has grown up, with Mikhail Bahktin as one of its foremost proponents. Attention to the importance of dialogue (and dialogic space, performance, and intertextuality) has come to occupy many narrative scholars. Summarizing current work in the field, Riessman (2008) comments 'meaning in the dialogic approach does not reside in a speaker's narrative, but in the dialogue between speaker and listener(s), investigator and transcript, and text and reader'.[25] A dialogic approach is built on the premise that communication between speaker and listener depends on a recognition of the inevitable tension between different locations and perspectives.

When we begin to think seriously about the viewpoint of another, one of the first things we must confront is our own otherness. In the words of Kapuściński, 'Everyone of us living on this planet is an Other in the view of Others'.[26] Thus it is that the imagination is not only vital to our attempt to penetrate the meaning-making system of another, but it is employed in our attempt to understand how we are viewed by them. We must imagine how we are imagined. One is reminded here of the haunting words of Scottish poet Robbie Burns: 'O would some power the giftie gie us to see ourselves as others see us'.[27] The more insight we have into the make-up of our own perception, the greater the possibility is that we will be able to see beyond that which we already know.

EVERYDAY IMAGINATION

'By reason and logic we die hourly, by imagination we live!' W. B Yeats proclaimed, thus resurrecting a binary which pits these most important faculties against one another.[28] And yet, the relationship between our powers to make sense of how the world operates (reason) and our inclination to be able to build other possibilities from this base (imagination) are not necessarily antithetical. Proud (2012) writes that this false dualism causes reason to become 'overlooked and unacknowledged. It takes a poet to understand reason... Reason is the mind's eye, able to judge and discern, but it is not harsh. Reason is gentle. Reason is sweet'.[29] The mind's eye, that which we can envision but which might not yet be, can be a most worthy guide in the journey to realising new possibilities.

In this book, the focus is on an imagination which does not leave the real world far behind but, rather, is grounded in it, which extends from the 'real', the world as we know it, to the world of the possible. It is imagination in its everyday guise, imagination as it is manifested as we think about our lives as they have been lived, and as they might be led, as we try to make sense of people who seem very different from ourselves, and even those with whom we think we share so much. Our imagination, in this sense, is not something which we dust off and put on for special occasions, a psychological tiara of sorts. Rather, it guides us from our waking hour to when we go to bed at night. It is with us always, sitting side by side with our reason and perception. Although it might be employed for constructing 'castles in the clouds', what concerns us in this volume is how we use it to transform our lives and our communities, for better or for worse. Like Stoetzler and Yuval-Davis, our starting position is that imagination is 'both individual and collective, self- as well as other-directed'.[30] It is our imagination which assists us in synthesizing the information we take in about the world around us, and helps us to process it, looking beyond and beneath what is.

The term everyday life is not one which is customarily combined with the word imagination. Rather, it has come to be associated with the seemingly banal minutiae of our existence. More than a century ago, Freud used the term in the title of his book, *The Psychopathology of Everyday Life*, which introduced the world to his theory of psychoanalysis. At approximately the same time, everyday life emerged as a key focus of social science research at the University of Chicago, in response to 'a need to understand the experiences of people living in the new big cities'.[31] Since that time, many scholars have turned their attention to this realm of existence: Lefebvre's *Critique of Everyday Life* (1947); Goffman's *The Presentation of Self in Everyday Life* (1959); and Certeau's *The Practice of Everyday Life* (1984) being but a few examples. By 1970, the concept of 'everyday life' had established itself as a subdiscipline of sociology. Writing at that time, Douglas asserts: 'sociology, like all disciplines that purport to be theoretical and applied sciences of human action, necessarily begins and ends with the understanding of everyday life'.[32] In the current postmodern era, the interest in everyday life has flourished[33-38]: society 'has been broken apart and reconstituted as everyday life'.[39] If we wish to understand our lives, we must, in the words of Clifford Geertz, 'descend into detail',[40] for 'Seeing heaven in a grain of sand is not a trick only poets can accomplish'.[41] Vital to this exploration for meaning is the narrative imagination, which holds the key to connecting the unique with the universal, the particular with the possible.

Let me now confess something. I never consciously set out to write a book about narrative imagination. Rather it was a topic which found me, and which would not accept being ignored. I have been engaged with narrative research of one kind or another for about a quarter of a century. In this time, I have explored a range of human experience, mostly through talking to people about their lives. This book is about where those conversations have taken me. Stepping back from the particulars of each research project,

I have come to realise that despite the apparent disparity of subject matter, in many ways I have found myself still hovering around the same territory, in the land which lies somewhere between the real and the possible.

In the chapters which follow, I explore how narrative and imagination come together in four specific arenas of life. Chapter 2 invites readers in to my own profession as an academic researcher. Using the metaphor of the performance of magic, the chapter examines those moments when we knowingly suspend disbelief and let ourselves travel to implausible, impossible places. As researchers, how do we balance the tension between our willingness to believe others—no matter how distant their experiences might be from our own—and critical detachment, even scepticism? Are there limits to how far we should be willing to travel into the worlds of others?

Chapter 3 develops the theme of 'imagining futures' with regard to how people think about their journey through the life course, and specifically their own aging. What narratives about age and aging are we surrounded by, and how do we map our own lives onto this projected storyline? Here I develop the idea of a 'blueprint for living,' examining where individuals acquire their ideas about aging and what contexts provoke meaningful consideration of where one is in relation to the self that one hopes to become. The chapter explores how different concepts of time are central to re-imagining the life course and our journey within it. What are the implications of not knowing when our lives will end—and that we will never narrate them once they are over? The chapter asks 'who tells stories about aging', and examines the potential of multiple generations telling stories of aging, looking forwards and backwards, from the cradle to the grave.

Chapter 4 focuses on the role of the narrative imagination in education, both in the classroom and beyond. Drawing on more than 25 years in the classroom, the chapter examines the stifling effect of current models of education on the ability of students and teachers to make connections between their formal learning and their lives, as they are and as they might be. The chapter poses fundamental pedagogical questions: What do we want our students/our children to learn and why? What can ignite curiosity, a desire to question, and to investigate? What is the relationship between learning about the world as it is and imagining ways of improving it?

Chapter 5 explores the role of imagination in political narratives, tracing the connections between personal narrative and social change. Using the case study of Obama's strategic use of stories, the chapter develops a theoretical model of political narratives, arguing for their central importance in analysing formal and informal politics. The chapter explores the changing life of national stories, examining how each generation re-invents for itself national narratives, re-positioning them within its own frames of reference and bestowing them with a revitalised sense purpose. The chapter considers the role of political narratives as a tool for re-imagining citizenship.

Chapter 6 reviews the relationship between narrative, imagination, and everyday life, in light of the discussion in the previous chapters. What, if anything, does suspending disbelief have to do with Obama's successful journey to the White House? What does our sense of our own aging have to do with how we interact with our students in the classroom? How does education for democratic citizenship affect the way in which individuals and groups experience themselves as being endowed with agency, potential forces for change in the social and political world? And what has all of this to do with a belief in the importance of articulating a vision of an alternative possibility?

Jerome Bruner's *Actual Minds, Possible Worlds*, published more than 25 years ago, remains one of the classic invitations to narrative inquiry. Its title directs us to the heart of the current investigation. In this book, he declares 'to be in the subjunctive mode is...to be trafficking in human possibilities rather than in settled certainties'.[42] Let us begin our journey into the subjunctive.

CHAPTER 2
Knowledge, Belief, and Disbelief

'...throughout history those who were closest to Imagination—poets, artists and visionaries—have believed it to be the deepest and sometimes the only source of knowledge' Jules Cashford writes. He continues: 'This knowledge exacts a total commitment, in contrast to knowledge gained by reasoning alone which is knowledge about something, not knowledge which changes you or which you have to change to know'.[1] What is the relationship between knowledge and imagination, particularly as it impacts on scholarly investigations of the social world? As already discussed in Chapter 1, our narrative imagination both synthesizes and deconstructs the knowledge we acquire from being in the world; thus, it helps us to bring together discordant entities, to perceive a new 'wholeness', a new reality or potential reality, just as it assists us in making the familiar strange. This dynamic creates a fundamental tension which lies at the heart of personal narrative research: a tension between a willingness to believe, to be transported to somewhere new, on the one hand, and a critical skepticism on the other, contradictory positions which often sit hand in hand, alternating turns of dominance at different moments in the research process.

It was while pondering this tension that I came to think about magic. I have always loved magic, and, indeed, as one of six children, I used to entertain my younger siblings for hours with a game my parents called 'Molly Magic'. How can I describe those hours spent in this unreal pursuit? I never went in for magic tricks as such; rather, it was my whole person which embodied the trick, for at the snap of my fingers I could become anyone. My brothers and I shared an entire world which was unknown to others, as I transformed myself to a whole range of characters, who would visit, then disappear, then visit again. Sometimes I would be a thief on the run, made breathless by my pursuers, seeking refuge beneath the beds of my brothers, and then, without warning, the then-I would disappear, being replaced by another I, this time the cop who was baffled and could not get his bearings. And on it would go, one story after another, after another. We spent hours, days, and weeks enveloped in these unraveling stories. Then new characters with different concerns would appear, and disappear. And so we spent much of our childhood, until one day one of my brothers, in a burst of anger, blurted out that he knew that I was wasn't 'really' magic. I had begun to suspect he thought this in any case, but such was our game that even I had convinced myself that in some way, these people did occupy my body. However, once my brother had made this declaration, the game was up. We could never reclaim the feeling of the time when he had believed, or had pretended to believe, in something which was clearly unbelievable.

How does this relate to interview-based narrative research? Asking people to tell you stories about themselves is, in some ways, akin to placing oneself in the role of an audience who is willing to suspend disbelief, to see with the mind's eye people who one will probably never meet, to smell, touch, taste and feel a world which one had not previously known. This is even true when the people and places which inhabit the stories one is hearing are in fact ones which the listener has also encountered in their own lives, recalling Heidegger's 'in wonder, what is most usual...becomes the most unusual'.[2] The same person is never the same person to two people, and neither is a place ever simply a place but, rather, something which is conjured up in memory, and as such changes character as it is constructed and reconstructed by different people and even by the same person over time.

However, the exchange between ourselves, as collectors of stories, and those who share with us accounts of their lives, only works so long as we are willing to believe. The moment we say, as my brother did to me, I don't believe you, the implicit contract is irreparably shattered. And because we intuitively sense that, we do not allow ourselves the indulgence of throwing down the gauntlet of disbelief, issuing the narrator with an overt challenge to provide us with better, more convincing evidence. We do not demand that they prove themselves, for in doing so we know that we will have crushed the delicate balance which enables telling of any kind. Life changes once our encounter with our narrators is finished, and we are not nearly so restrained. Indeed, it is the tool of our trade, the sign of a knowledgeable scholar, that we burst our bubble of suspended disbelief. The act of analysis demands both a critical distance, as well as some measure of engaged attachment. In being critical, we release ourselves from operating within the framework of truth into which our narrator has invited us, a framework which lends not only coherence but also meaning to the stories they have shared with us. With our skeptic's eye, we dismantle the walls of the imaginary world which has been constructed for us and by us. It is this ongoing movement between our believing and disbelieving which marks us as scholars., But when and why are we willing to believe some implausible accounts and not others?

MAGIC AND SOCIAL BELIEFS

> The fakir drew from under his knee a ball of gray twine. Taking the loose end between his teeth, with a quick upward motion, tossed the ball into the air. Instead of coming back to him it kept on going up and up until out of sight and there remained only the long swaying end... [A] boy about six years old... walked over to the twine and began climbing it... The boy disappeared when he had reached a point thirty or forty feet from the ground... A moment later the twine disappeared.[3]

These words, published in the *Chicago Tribune* in 1890, were nothing more than a desperate attempt to increase [the newspaper's] circulation. [4] And yet, here, in this fabricated piece of writing, lie the origins of a trick, which, though never performed, has become 'the world's most famous illusion'.[5]

Peter Lamont's book, *The Rise of the Indian Rope Trick: The Biography of a Legend*, tells a remarkable tale, which is both a detailed account of the history of this particular magic trick, as well as a gripping psychological read. Ultimately, the book is about what makes something believable, even when it is evidently false. We know that people cannot be suspended in midair, neither 40 nor even 4 feet from the ground. And yet people could somehow convince themselves that this had happened. Indeed, an entire industry has developed around this mythical construction.

So how was it, then, that this clearly impossible feat not only became transformed into something that was at least in theory believable—that is, people were prepared to believe the accounts of others that they had witnessed such an event? And how, over time, did Chicago become transposed into the deep forests of darkest India? Lamont's history of this trick is engaging precisely because it traces the development of social imagination. What people are willing to believe depends to a great extent on their framework of reference. Magic is intricately tied to the social imagination, and what is captivating for a group in one particular place and time may be significantly less so for others. In this way, one can see that magic operates as a social barometer, providing an indicator not only of what is accepted as

Figure 2.1:
The Indian rope trick was created as a hoax of a Chicago journalist, and yet metamorpho-sised into a symbol of 'exotic India' where all things are possible. When are we willing to suspend disbelief?

fact, but it also charts a construction of reality which is potentially accept-able, in other words, the world of the possible, if not-yet real.

Lamont explains that as the rope trick, or, more accurately, talk about the rope trick, developed, its place of origin changed from the American Midwest to Asia, simply because of generally held Western views about the exotic East. For many who would hear the tale of the young boy suspended high up in the air, such a thing could only happen in a place shrouded in mystery, where the ordinary rules of physics did not apply.

> For the British, the East in general, and India in particular, was becoming a place of romance and mystery, providing the magic that was lacking in the West.... [The image of the East as a place of wonder] was based on the idea that magic was not merely unexplained but inexplicable, that magic might be real. In

the modern West, this idea could be entertained only in relation to an imagined India, a far-off place where different rules might apply.[6]

Lamont is rather philosophical about how and why people imagine the things that they do. Magic, he says, is 'a way of getting at how people imagine their own world, and part of the world that's not their own'.[7] Throughout our lives, we identify who we are by defining who we are not, and we do this through stories we construct about ourselves, and about 'others'. How we imagine otherness, and how we do and don't relate that to the world which is familiar to us, are everyday processes of identity negotiation. And so, coming back to the question of why the Indian rope trick became transplanted to India, Lamont comments: 'With the notion of the mystic East that the West has, the people in the West may find an inexplicable mystery in India somehow more impressive, more mysterious, more mystical than a similar mystery at home, because India has this air of mystery to people from the West...'[8] In other words, the impossible was deemed possible because the unlikely was placed into a context where unusual and strange things were thought to occur as part of the everyday.

Another interesting example which illustrates this is the fate of the Sawing Through a Woman act. This trick, well known to modern audiences, was first publicly performed at the Finsbury Park Empire on January 17, 1921.[9] The illusionist was P. T. Selbit. It is most interesting to note that before this time, 'it was not a cliché that pretty ladies were teased and tortured by magicians'.[10] Indeed, it was usually young men who performed the roles of the terrified victims. This trick was different, however, as it required a particular flexibility and small frame in order to be successfully carried out. Thus it was that Selbit broke with tradition, and had a woman in this role. This would prove to be the secret of his success.

When Selbit first auditioned the act for the great magician Nevil Maskelyne at St. George's Hall, his act was turned down. For Maskelyne, the act did not impress, and he failed to appreciate the impact that it would come to have. For as it happened, others did observe the act that day, and hired Selbit; and from there was born 'the perfect product for the decade which would be later said to roar: impulsive, aggressive and thrilling'.[11] But why did it make such a hit? Steinmeyer hazards a guess here: 'for some reason, at that time and place, it was suddenly entertaining to victimize a young lady on the stage. Selbit, perhaps quite innocently, had come upon the right idea for the right time'.[12] It is not incidental to the success of this trick that the victim was a woman. When the trick was performed using a boy as the victim, it failed to produce the same reaction from the audience.

Only two years had passed since the end of World War I when Selbit first introduced this trick to the public. In his trick, 'no blood was shed, no unpleasantries exposed within the box and the magical finale revealed a lady unharmed'.[13] (Selbit did, however, appeal to blood and gore in drumming up trade, as we will see later) In some sense, the trick allowed the audience to escape into a world of unreality, and a world in which one who appears to have been killed is in fact alive and well by the end. But there was another political influence which proved to be possibly even more important, and that was the rise of the woman's suffrage movement. In Britain in 1905, the Women's Vote Bill failed, and the Women's Social and Political Union was formed. Though the First World War caused a lull in the movement, because of the shortage of men on the home front, many women began to perform what had hitherto been considered 'men's work' in the public sphere, and women received partial voting rights (i.e., for women over 30) the same year the war ended. (It was not until 1928 that all women over 21 could vote).

Selbit did all sorts of things to increase the general appeal of his sawing trick, but one of the most interesting was employing the suffragette Christabel Pankhurst, who was regarded by many as a terrorist, to act as the woman to be sawed in half. The Magic Circle's official publication

Figure 2.2:
'Sawing a Woman in Half' Show. Elaborate measures were adopted to attract business, including pouring buckets of stage blood on the streets and parking an ambulance outside of the venue where the trick was being performed.

Figure 2.3:
'Sawing Through'. The famous suffragette Christabel Pankhurt, was paid £20 a week to act as the woman sawed in two. Magic is always deeply embedded in the culture in which it is performed.

proclaimed 'To offer Christabel Pankhurst £20 a week as a permanent sawing block, that was genius'.[14] The scene outside the venue where Pankhurst was sawed in two night after night, was utter pandemonium: 'ambulances chased back and forth with sirens blaring, while stage hands drenched the gutters with buckets of stage blood. When Ms. Pankhurst was finally sawed in half, the crowd went wild'.[15] The results were sensational, as people queued around the block to be able to get tickets. As one writer comments: 'It was as if the suffragettes had frightened society, and magic was, literally, putting them back in their box'.[16]

As Nevil Maskelyne observed nearly a century ago, 'Like all else in the world, magic cannot stand still. It must either advance with the times, or fall behind them'. Both the Indian Rope Trick and the Sawing a Woman Trick illustrate that magic is indeed a product of a particular moment in history; a magic trick only 'works' if it can speak to the popular imagination, and this imagination is always contextually situated.

THE PSYCHOLOGY OF MAGIC

What people are and are not willing to believe, and what contextual factors contribute to this, relates not only to considerations of logic and probability, but also to a wider sense of social expectations and attitudes. Thus, not only does good magic rely on good psychology, but psychologists can learn much about the operations of the mind by studying situations in which magic is performed.

French psychologist Alfred Binet, most well known for the development of the IQ test, was fascinated by magic, and in particular the magician's use of suggestion to accomplish his results. Binet published an article on the psychology of magic in 1893, and Richard Wiseman, a psychologist and accomplished magician, has uncovered archival footage[17] showing what is now believed to be the first moving image of a magician, which was the product of collaboration between Binet, the Parisian photographer Georges Demeny—a pioneer in 'chronophotography', forerunner of modern day cinema—and a French magician by the name of Raynaly. The 'film' is in fact a series of 23 still images which show the 'disappearance' of a ball. What is interesting here is not so much the trick itself, but rather Binet's fascination with it.

Binet had been interested in the mechanics of conjuring, and in fact had invited five magicians to come to his laboratory, in order that he could observe them as they performed.[18] Binet's critical question concerned what led audiences to be receptive to 'seeing' illusions. Susan Lachapelle (2008) argues that despite secrecy being critical for their profession, the magicians accepted Binet's invitation because they saw themselves as men of science, and wished to gain respect as such.[19]

More than 100 years later, psychologists continue to regard magic as a vehicle for understanding aspects of the human mind. Although magic has been around for a very long time, Wiseman comments that we are only now

> starting to realise that magicians have a lot of implicit knowledge about how we perceive the world around us because they have to deceive us in terms of controlling attention, exploiting the assumptions we make when we do and don't notice a change in our environment... Magicians are manipulating your consciousness. They are showing you something impossible... They're getting you to construct a narrative, which simply isn't true. So that means they know how to make you aware of certain things and blind to others.[20]

Wiseman believes that magic 'will give us a real insight into the deep mysteries of consciousness'; ultimately, consciousness is only 'a construction, and may even be an illusion'[21]: we fool ourselves into believing that we have an awareness, an alertness about the physical reality about us, but this awareness is at best imperfect, because we 'see' what is not there, and don't see what is. In as much as consciousness is about perceiving a relationship between one's self and one's environment, magic illustrates that our awareness can be manipulated and we can be made to 'misperceive' in predictable ways, for instance by misdirection of attention, upon which much magic depends.

Gustav Kuhn, a magician and psychologist, argues that magic is 'the trick to understanding the human mind'[22]; magic provides us with a an insight into the complexity of human perception. His basic argument is that we 'see' what we expect to see, which does not always correspond to the physical reality we encounter:

> Our visual representation of the world is much more impoverished than we would assume. People can be looking at something without being aware of it. Perception doesn't just involve looking at an object but attending to it.... Much of the picture in our head of our surroundings is a massive construction, based on expectations, what we think is important, what we normally encounter, and so on. And that's what magicians are very good at exploiting.[23]

Kuhn and his colleagues have conducted a number of experiments which pinpoint critical moments when people do not see what is before them. In one of these experiments, a lighter and cigarette 'disappear' into thin air, an effect which is achieved through what is known as misdirection, the 'diversion of attention away from its method'[24] so that the audience is not aware of what is being done before their very eyes, because their attention is being diverted elsewhere.

Kuhn argues that, just as human cognition 'relies on assumptions about the world... [which are] often correct [but] they sometimes are not', so much magic relies on expectations which conjurers can manipulate. Moreover, he argues that 'illusions created by the conjurer are not that different from the tricks the mind plays on us in everyday life, which most of the time go unnoticed'.[25] To illustrate this point, Kuhn and his colleagues offer the example of the perception of colour, which is always influenced by the colour of surrounding objects. It turns out that seeing may be over-rated as an indicator of what we should believe.

The art of deception

Deception is part of everyday life. Indeed, Wiseman (2007) reports research showing that 'most people tell about two important lies each day, [and] that a third of conversations involve some form of deception'.[26] Deceiving, and being deceived is not, in fact, very unusual. Magic, however, presents us with a special case of this everyday activity. As Peter Lamont comments:

> Deception is used by everybody, everyday, and there are specific types of deception which require special expertise. What magicians do, which is almost unique in deception, is that they deceive people when the people know they are being deceived. In other forms of deception, the whole point is that you don't know you are being deceived. If you are a conman, if you are lying to your wife, or your school teacher, or it's a military deception, it's always about the person that you are deceiving being unaware that they are being deceived.[27]

This special form of 'knowing deception', in which two parties share similar expectations that one will deceive and the other will be deceived, is key to the performance of magic. In order for this to be accomplished, however, the magician must have given considerable thought to how people think. 'Any serious magician has a theory about how to deceive his or her audience. If this theory is wrong, the magic trick will fail and the audience will spot the secret'.[28] But what is it that renders certain acts of deception more likely to succeed than others? How is it that conjurers are able to bring their audiences with them, despite the obvious fact that what they are purporting to do is impossible? Three key elements contribute to the likelihood of the deception going undetected: (1) the performance of the conjurer, (2) attention to detail and setting, and (3) the disposition of the audience.

Clearly, a magician is most likely to bring others into her world of illusion if she appears to believe in it herself. She must be able to offer her audience a convincing performance, to demonstrate to them with conviction and authority that, indeed, the impossible is possible, physical reality can be bent, the laws of physics can be suspended, and, thus, she affirms for them that there is much more to life than that which we know, understand, and can explain. A precondition for getting others to believe the impossible is for the conjurer to (apparently) believe herself, accomplished in part by believing *in* herself and the 'truth' of what she is showing to others.

In psychology's earliest years as a discipline, there was much interest in the psychology of deception.[29] Dessoir, one of the leading psychologists at the turn of the century, was, like many of his colleagues, fascinated by what makes conjuring work. He argued that 'anyone could purchase books and instructions from magic dealers. But knowing the mechanics and details of the trick neither protects you from being fooled by it, nor enables you successfully to perform it'.[30] Rather, he argued, the secret lay in what he called the 'psychological kernel', 'the ability to convince spectators that you really hold an orange in your left hand when it actually remains in your right'.[31] In sum, he argued, 'Only he who is convinced, convinces'.[32]

Robert-Houdin described a magician as 'an actor playing the part of a magician',[33] again, emphasizing the importance of behaving as if you believe that what you are doing is true. Max Maven, American magician and mentalist, has even created a magician character, which he has played on a number of different magic-related television series. Maven, who has also been a 'magic consultant' for some of the biggest names in magic in our time, believes that many magicians are in fact 'afraid of creating a truly magical effect'.[34] However, when the actor/magician exudes a belief in herself and in the magic she is performing, the audience 'become involved and experience the event rather than observe... If acting is not right, the audience will remain detached from the event'.[35]

The second key ingredient for believability is that of the attention to detail and setting. Jasper Maskelyne (son of Nevil Maskelyne, mentioned earlier) and David Devant dominated the English magic scene in the early part of the 20th century. In World War II, Maskelyne would put his expertise to use in the war effort, when, as a member of the Magic Gang, he created large-scale illusions of warships and tanks. He also managed to conceal Alexandria and the Suez Canal, in order to misdirect German bombers. His secret to success? 'Let every accessory and incidental detail be kept "within the picture," and in harmony with the general impression which is intended to be conveyed'.[36] If even the smallest of details seems somehow wrong to the audience, the seed of doubt will have been planted, and it is most likely that the perception of not only the trick, but of the entire performance, will have been affected. And not only must the details of the trick be attended to, but equally important is the setting in which the magic comes to life. Simply put, the magic must be seen to be naturally part of the context in which it is performed. In the words of Jim Steinmeyer: 'The art of the magician is not found in the simple deception, but in what surrounds it, the construction of a reality which supports the illusion'.[37]

The third vital ingredient is, of course, the willingness of an audience to suspend their disbelief. As magician Jamie Raven comments: 'When you tell people you are a magician you are laying down a challenge. 'You're telling them "I am going to lie to you"'.[38] This is an unusual situation in that presumably people have voluntarily placed themselves in a context in which they wish to be deceived—that is what they have paid their money for. Generally speaking, most people in the audience will want the magic to 'work'. Indeed, were the means of trickery obvious, they would feel let down, and might even ask for their money to be returned. '...what motivates people to let magicians mess with their minds? After all, there is a fundamental problem with this relationship. At the end of the day, you are paying someone, to deceive you; you are twice the sucker'.[39]

So why do we do it?

IMAGINATION AND CULTURE

Paul Harris, a magician and one of the technical advisors for David Blaine, has described what he sees as the fundamental lure of magic: it is our desire to be astonished. Astonishment, he argues, is our natural state, and can be commonly observed in childhood. However, it is mostly lost in the adult years. People are attracted to magic, Harris argues, because it returns them to that state.[40] Peter Lamont, whose work on the Indian rope trick was discussed earlier, says he finds Harris' way of thinking about magic the most convincing. He then elaborates on this:

> ... when you are born, your mind is kind of blank. You don't know what's possible, you don't know what's impossible, and the whole world is wonderful. As one grows older, we get more and more fixed about what is possible, and we have boxes that we put everything into. We forget that these boxes are things that we construct. They are not reality, but simply our construction of reality. What magic does is provide an experience that does not fit into the box.[41]

What and how we imagine possibilities is integrally connected to how we perceive reality. As magic shows, human perception is always partial and often malleable. A number of magicians have commented that they take much of their inspiration from the everyday. And as Lamont's discussion of the Indian rope trick illustrated, what people are willing to believe has much to do with how they imagine what they do not know. Magic tricks work because we are attached to reality as we expect it to be. As the great magician Joseph Jastrow observed more than 100 years ago:

> We are creatures of the average; we are adjusted for the most probable event; our organism has acquired the habits impressed upon it by the most frequent experiences; and this has induced an inherent logical necessity to interpret a new experience by the old, an unfamiliar by the familiar.[42]

Magician Arthur Trace, when asked what he does to refresh his mind, responds 'I go to my local coffee shop and daydream, and just listen and take a good look around me. Inspiration comes from many different sources. I try to keep my mind open to any inspiration by being aware of what's around me'.[43]

In fact, as magician Jim Steinmeyer comments, 'There are few secrets that [magicians] possess which are beyond a grade school science class, little technology more complex than a rubber band, a square of black fabric or a length of thread'.[44] In other words, magic magnifies reality as we know it, takes the everyday and renders it strange and exotic to us. We as the audience receive the magic as 'other', whose operating features are entirely different to those from the world we know. One reason for the enduring success of magic through the ages is our deep-rooted desire to look over the edge of the boundaries of possible. But as imagination is a property of both individuals and cultures, what seems unthinkable in one context might indeed be regarded as rather ordinary in another.

CONSIDERING THE UNBELIEVABLE IN SCHOLARLY RESEARCH

What insights can we glean from the present discussion—on the willingness to believe the impossible, the art of deception, and the situated nature of imagination—which might benefit us as we pursue our research, asking people to tell us stories of their lives, and trying to make sense of things which we might never have experienced and may well find hard to believe, even to imagine? Because the purpose of this chapter has been to stimulate thinking about how we approach stories which are different to those with which we are familiar—and so, in that sense, believable—I would like to present my thoughts here in the format of three inter-related questions to think with.

How should we approach critical moments in our interviews when a leap of faith is required? Scholars receive years of training in critical thinking, which teaches us how to uncover layers of meaning, and to detect inconsistencies in patterns of thought, and information provided. Very often, in-depth conversations with others require us to suspend that critical thinking if we are to try to enter into the world they are assembling before us. This demands that we take seriously the story another shares with us. Personal narratives represent a personal truth, or truths, even if that truth does not coincide with reality.

What role does deception play in the narrative encounter? As researchers, we seek to evaluate the truthfulness of accounts which are offered to us. There are a number of indicators which we measure to evaluate how convinced we are (which is why the role of the narrator is akin to the magician: only s/he who is convinced is convincing.) And yet, we know that all accounts are only ever partial, and that narrators cast themselves in particular roles, depending on who they perceive as being their audience. Personal stories which they tell us function as a means of securing that identity, and of obscuring others. However, as researchers we are also engaged in this form of everyday deception, sometimes explicitly (as is the case when we fail to reveal the true topic of our research), but more often implicitly, by not making clear our own personal allegiances, antipathies, and priorities. We also are deceived by ourselves, when we hear only that which we expect to hear; anticipated storylines serve as a misdirection in interviews, equally effective to those employed in magic tricks.

How do we construct the limits of the possible, and when are we willing to suspend/extend these boundaries? One of the primary the filters through which we process stories we hear is by asking ourselves 'could this really happen'? If what we hear deviates too significantly from what we ourselves have encountered, either through our own experience or that of others we know, or through other sources of social knowledge, then we are likely to question the veracity of the account. One understands that a story in which the narrator reports 'floating on air' either occurs where there is no gravity, or else is only true in a metaphorical sense, and should be interpreted as a description of an emotional state. But when the content of the narrative is not so easily disproved, for instance in trauma testimony, the listener is faced with a difficult challenge. The fact that some atrocities are 'unthinkable' does not mean they have not occurred. Erika Apfelbaum has written about the 'threatening implications of listening' to traumatic testimony, which, she says, 'requires a willingness to follow the teller into a world of radical otherness and to accept the frightening implications it carries for our personal lives and society as a whole'.[45] And even in a less dramatic context, how can we ensure that we do not put on to others feelings that we imagine we might experience in such a context, but for which the narrator offers no evidence? In other words, how can we respect the difference between who they are and who we are?

In my experience, we are often unwilling to extend the boundaries of what we regard as believable, and yet, if we are to do our research well, then we are required to do so. This is why research of this nature is so emotionally demanding, for ultimately we must be willing to take seriously that the way we see the world is only one way amongst infinite possibilities, to recognise the situatedness of knowledge and of interpretation. Our research teaches us that 'whatever set and scenario we construct on the main floor of our experience, there remain at the bottom of the stairs such dilemmas and ambiguities of social and personal life, such shape-shifting, as to offer no permanent resolution good for all seasons'.[46]

I have written before about the relationship between research and desire:

> Most often, the questions which guide our research originate from deep within
> ourselves. We care about the topics we explore—indeed, we care very much.
> While our projects may be presented with an appearance of professional detach-
> ment, most of us most of the time are personally invested in the research we
> undertake. Our chosen areas of expertise mean something to us; there is a rea-
> son we examine the questions we do. Sometimes we might even feel that our
> questions choose us; they occur to us (sometimes, arriving almost impercepti-
> bly, other times like a thunderbolt) but then will not go away.[47]

We are then not indifferent to what we uncover in the course of our
research, our 'findings'. Even while we may pursue our scholarship with
rigor, and feel that we are not only intellectually but also ethically obliged
to pursue leads which may undermine our own inclinations, still we come
to our research with a particular sense of purpose.

Questioning the purpose of what we as academics are doing is not only a
recent concern. How we know what we know and why that is of any import
are queries which can be traced back to the earliest days of philosophy,
though each age must articulate these questions in terms relevant to its
own time. The question posed in 1939 by Robert Lynd, the American soci-
ologist, in the title to his book *Knowledge for What?* is ultimately one for
all researchers. What is the larger project that we hope the knowledge we
generate will contribute towards?

Lynd criticized social scientists for hiding behind their precocious beards
of 'dispassionate research' and 'scientific objectivity'. The plea for hands-on
engagement with problems of the real world is one which has been voiced
again and again by academics in the 75 years since the publication of Lynd's
book. Far from remaining outside and 'untainted' by the social problems
they observe, some social scientists feel there is a duty incumbent upon
them to make a stand, answering loud and clear to the question posed in
the title to Howard Becker's article, published more than four decades ago,
'Whose side are we on'.[48] Becker's argument concerns questions of perspective and accountability. He writes:

> We must always look at the matter from someone's point of view. The scientist
> who proposes to understand society must...get into the situation enough to
> have a perspective on it. And it is likely that his [sic] perspective will be greatly
> affected by whatever positions are taken by any or all of the other participants

in that varied situation. Almost all the topics that sociologists study, at least those that have some relation to the real worlds around us, are seen by society as morality plays and we shall find ourselves, will-nilly, taking part in those plays on one side or the other.[49]

However, there are a number of questions which arise in relation to this argument. The one which concerns us here is the problem of the pronoun—who is the 'we' to whom Becker refers?

> One can no longer assume that 'we' know who 'we' are. Equally, we can no longer feel so comfortable in knowing who 'they' the 'others' are either. The question of partisanship and alignment is ever more pressing, but its social and ethical configuration is more complex...It becomes increasingly difficult to discern 'sides' while increasingly acceptable to be committed to taking sides of some sort. The methodological and ethical terrain has become more fragmented. While it has become more overtly politicized, the lines of political commitment and affiliation have become less distinct.[50]

There is a certain 'taken-for-granted-ness' of the categories into which we place ourselves and others which cannot be supported by closer scrutiny. We are not all of us the same puzzle, even while we may share some pieces in common.

This has important and concrete implications for research such as my own, which often probes a rocky political psychological landscape. Although it is tempting to assume that like-mindedness on one issue is a strong indicator of the same on another issue, I have learned time and again that this is not necessarily so. In the 25 years since I have been talking to people about their political worldviews, I have from time to time encountered what I now call 'inconvenient data'—that is, those things which I (1) did not anticipate that my participants would say, and (2) wish they hadn't. I have not always been able to see or hear what is being said, so focused was I on the story I was expecting to hear. In the language of magic tricks, my attention was misdirected.

Let me give an example. The following exchange comes from an interview I conducted as part of a study on lifetime socialist activists. All the people who participated in this study were, for me, something akin to personal heroes, having fought for social justice for at least half a century. In an interview with Marge, we were talking about her political commitment in the 1950s. I asked her if Khrushchev's admission of the excesses of Stalin had caused her to re-evaluate any of her beliefs.

> Marge: I agreed with Stalin, I agreed with Stalin. We'll never get socialism through ballot box—do you think we will?

Molly: Well, I don't know...

Marge: I don't think so, I don't think we'll get socialism through ballot box... 'he's killed millions' they're only just finding out that he's killed a million. At time he never killed a million. It's all a tale. Propaganda is very powerful you know, and the propaganda they've against the Soviet Union is very powerful.

What I find most striking about this exchange is my own reaction. Did I really not have an opinion about the importance of democracy ('socialism through ballot box')? When Marge continues to deny that Stalin 'killed millions' I was simply stunned. Indeed, this piece of 'inconvenient data' stayed buried for decades; I could not write about it, I could barely bring myself to think about it.

Years later, I have come to regard such encounters (and there have been others) as ripe with potential. In these ruptures, there is much to sort through, and the emotional and intellectual difficulty of doing so is well worth the effort. I believe that we must return to the question which Lynd set: What is the knowledge for? In terms of conducting interviews, we as researchers need to evaluate what exactly we see as being the purpose of the encounter. Is our purpose to persuade, document, understand, give voice to, a combination of these, or none, something else entirely? And when we do encounter these unexpected turnings, how should we engage with them? Is our work morally compromised if we fail to challenge points of view which we find reprehensible? Embracing the principle that all knowledge is situated, I can make sense of what Marge is saying in the preceding excerpt, even while I cannot accept it. But it is important to take her point of view seriously, and it requires not only historical consciousness, but also imagination—and a strong stomach—to do so. The narrative imagination, Jens Brockmeier surmises, '...compels us to imagine what is not the self, what is the Other, the uncharted terrain—and what's more, to familiarize the strange'.[51] This is my challenge as I try to make sense of a worldview, such as Marge's, which is both similar to, and very different from, my own.

Another, and very different example, can be found in the work of Siyanda Ndlovu, a young South African scholar who has researched the complex meaning of blackness. He explicitly locates himself within this exploration, describing the effects of his early years on the formation of the person he was to become: 'The place of my past, the place of my childhood, the place I call home: the township'.[52] Despite growing up in the township—'an apartheid invention to separate whites from blacks'—it was, in fact, coming to Manchester, England, where he had his first conscious experience of 'feeling black'. He writes:

It was one of those defining moments in my life where I felt completely out of place, sticking out like a sore thumb. One day I decided to walk around the city by myself and the strangest feeling came over me. I felt black. I am, and have always been, conscious of the colour of my skin. This should come as no surprise given South Africa's particular history. But this was a different feeling; walking the streets of Manchester was a particularly interesting and strange experience... in the midst of all those 'white' bodies, every single time I saw another black face, black body, my heart skipped a beat. There was an immediate identification on my part. He/she is 'like me.' They look like me; I am like them. I belong!... Racial difference... is not a neutral entity as it carries with it history and politics.[53]

Ndlovu describes himself as being 'interested in those moments when you learn that your skin is connected to a long history of oppression',[54] and yet he powerfully resists the inclination towards any form of essentialism. (Here, he illustrates his argument with a story about being with a group of young people and feeling an unsaid affinity with those with whom he shared his race, until the moment that he realised they were homophobic). He writes about the complexity of racial identity:

When people recognize me as black, I get offended! Is black the only thing they see? Foregrounding my blackness is painful in all sorts of ways. "You are black." This is a kind of putting me in my place lest I forget the colour of my skin and lest I think that I am part of the 'in' (read, white) group. On the other hand, *when people claim not to see or not to recognise my blackness*, I am equally deeply offended! How can you not see the colour of my skin? It is most visible and undeniably and irrefutably the first thing you see. My blackness may not matter to you, but do not say that you cannot *see* it. Interesting paradox, I think. But, it could be a productive space, working through and with the apparent contradiction, as opposed to wishing it away (Italics in original).[55]

So what does this very rich account of the meaning of blackness bring to the discussion of magic? Firstly, Ndlovu argues strongly that race is a social invention; at the same time, he writes of 'the "real" effects that the historical construct of "race" has on my life, experiences, interpersonal relationships and identity'.[56,57] How we make sense of the world around us is influenced by the web of social meanings in which we ourselves are embedded. Although we have come to assume that in some sense the world is objectively real, this 'reality' can be re-imagined, and thus re-constructed. Ndlovu's account is not limited to his own embodied sense of being black, but it certainly includes it. He identifies a paradox, arguing the challenge which it presents should be worked through, not ignored: 'Difference' he tells us, 'is not something to be feared or erased but rather engaged'. As a white woman from a very different, and markedly more privileged background than Ndlovu, my sense is that a genuine appreciation of this powerful argument demands that I recognise the limitations of my ability to know the experience from which he speaks. I know, that '[my] white body, is not a neutral entity'[58]—it is a critical component of the (very partial) position from which I see, and do not see, the world. And yet I also know that acknowledging this difference is a first step towards creating a forum in which new ways of knowing and imagining become possible.

MAGIC AND THE BEYOND

As social researchers, we continually explore the relationship between what is ('reality') and what might be ('the possible'). We need legends, enchantment, wonderment, and astonishment to help us extend our conceptual world. For a magic trick to work, individuals must be willing to be transported beyond the here and now, beyond the scientifically known and knowable world, into a world of new and often improbable possibilities. In order to immerse myself in a world very different from the one I know, I, as a researcher, must be willing to suspend my disbelief, and to follow the paths of the narratives which are told and performed before me in the course of my investigations.

Indeed, we researchers have a thing or two to learn from magicians, whose successful performance depends on exploring experiences that do not, in the words of Peter Lamont 'fit into the box':

> ....at the moment when something disappears, or appears, or changes, at that point you are seeing something, which your experience tells cannot be possible. And the boxes that you have disappear for a moment.... That's a real moment of wonder. That's where you say perhaps there is more to the world than what you see. It doesn't have to be a real miracle. It just reminds you in your day-to-day life what you don't get reminded [of very] often. The way you live your life is just one way. The way you look at the world is just one way.[59]

Not so long ago I had the privilege of being in a small audience where David Blaine was speaking. When he entered the room, it was as if we were on a Hollywood set; immediately the entire place erupted in spontaneous and prolonged applause, something akin to the adulation directed towards rock-n'-roll stars, only different. There was excitement in the air, mixed with anticipation. What would he do, what would he say? This most practiced and disciplined of performers did not disappoint. He began by signalling to the empty pitcher placed in front of him, and asked what he had to do to get a drink of water. Without skipping a beat, he then turned and produced from his own mouth several gallons of clear liquid into the pitcher; he then poured himself a glass and drank. One woman sitting in the front row squealed, which was grist to the mill, and he offered her some 'water' as well. She declined. And so the evening continued.

What was most engaging for me was how he spoke about his craft. When the floor was opened to questions, I was able to ask him about the role of imagination in performing magic. He paused and said quite simply that in order to perform a 'trick' you had to be able to imagine that there are other possible realities from the ones we know; he declared himself in that sense to 'believe in magic'. As the event ended, David Blaine invited members of the audience to come and talk with him, and to have their photos taken if they wanted. I dutifully obliged, and got in the queue. But then something quite unbelievable happened—he picked me out of the queue to have my photo taken alone with him (all the others were to be in groups of 8 or so). There we were, arm in arm, smiling for the cameras. And then I left. Later it occurred to me that maybe, just maybe, one day he would show that photo to someone, boasting that he had met the woman of Molly Magic fame. For that one night at least I believed that anything was possible.

CHAPTER 3

Ageing

One of the first, and last, places that the question of imagination enters into our everyday thinking is in our conceptualization of the passage of time in our own lives, in other words our aging. In the first chapter, I discussed the way in which narrative imagination is used as a vehicle for accessing the world of 'the other'. This has a particular relevance in discussions of aging. Because there is so much emphasis placed upon youth culture, there is little attention which is given to the selves we hope to grow in to, the selves we are becoming. Rarely are we asked to articulate our visions for a meaningful old age, in general, and for ourselves personally.

SITUATING OURSELVES

Some years ago, a woman I knew quite well, who was in her mid-80s, used to refer to 'the old folks', a group from which she always excluded herself. One day, she had a fall in the middle of the road, and was horrified that strangers came to help her. She was not, she insisted, old nor in need of any assistance. She repeated this story several times, and with each telling those who came to her aid were made to look increasingly most unreasonable. The possibility that she had fallen because of any fragility was more bruising to her than the physical wound which resulted from the fall. The incident only augmented her determination not to identify herself as an old person, who was in need of some kind of help.

In fact, distancing oneself from being perceived as being a member of a stigmatized group, as this woman was so insistent to do, is not unusual. There are many very rational reasons why such a strategy makes sense, and indeed it lies at the heart the politics of 'passing'; who amongst us does not feel complimented to hear that we do not look our age? Why is it that we work so hard to distance ourselves from the skin in which we live?

One of the most important first steps in exploring the role of imagination in our constructions of aging is to locate ourselves within this framework. On the occasions when aging is spoken about, it is often as a property belonging to other people. References to our own aging tend to be in relation to topics such as reduced fitness, memory loss ('senior moments'), and thickening waistlines. But all of us, from the moment we are born, are aging, and when we stop aging we will cease to exist. Aging is a central thread across a human lifetime. Yet, if this is so, why is it that information about our age is often regarded as something which is, and should be, kept private? Our silence is also our complicity.

It has been noted by many that ageism is an unusual axis of marginalization, as it discriminates against a group to which all of us have the potential to belong. Every time we wait for a red light to turn green before crossing the road, or try to give up smoking, we are at some level trying to ensure that we have the luxury of reaching our promised three score and ten years. In this sense, 'ageism differs from other forms of systemic injustice, like racism or classism, because everyone will be subjected to its injuries unless significant change comes to pass. It is in our self-interest, and not only for the sake of others' well-being, to combat it'.[1] As Simone de Beauvoir commented more than 40 years ago:

> We look at the image of our own future provided by the old [and] we do not believe it: an absurd inner voice whispers that *that* will never happen to us— when *that* happens it will no longer be ourselves that it happens to. Until the moment it is upon us, old age is something that only affects other people.[2]

If we do safely make it across the street and nothing else thwarts us in our efforts to stay alive, then *that* really will happen to us; indeed, the seeds for its happening have been planted at the moment of our birth. So it behooves us to locate ourselves in this story of aging, this story which is not only about humankind, but also about ourselves.

The very act of narrating our own age can be a small act of resistance. If what we see (and fail to see) has to do with our vantage point, then surely our age makes some sort of difference (though not necessarily a determining one). Our age is relevant—so why is it that it so rarely features when we tell stories about our adult lives? Bill Bytheway captures the balance between continuity and change which is implicit in the aging process.

...getting real about age entails recognising that ageing is constant, complex and slow. And that it does make a difference to our lives and our relations with others, despite the unchanging continuity implicit in our fixed personal identities, and the apparently constant regeneration of many of the social worlds we live in. We have to learn to cope with the idea that each of us is still and, at the same time, no longer the person we used to be. It is through sensitive and imaginative social research that we will gain a better understanding of this conundrum.[3]

That we are 'still and at the same time no longer the person we used to be' is a statement that applies to all of us, as we live in and through time; who we are is marked by both an 'unchanging continuity' as well as a 'constant regeneration'. Simone de Beauvoir identifies the 'basic truth of life' as a recognition of the fact that: '...life is an unstable system in which balance is continually lost and continually recovered: it is inertia that is synonymous with death. Change is the law of life'.[4]

Many of those who study aging fail to situate themselves in relation to their investigations. As Bytheway comments, much gerontological scholarship implies 'that it is produced by ageless gerontologists researching their "age-ful," "elderly" subjects'.[5] Addressing this issue, Bytheway points to the keynote address to the British Society of Gerontology delivered by social campaigner Margaret Simey, when she was well into her 80s. 'For us, "we" are older people and gerontologists are "them"' she told her audience.[6]

Still, aging is a process we all know something about: We have been doing it all our lives. Baars identifies a peculiarly human paradox: '[A]ll human beings are constantly aging, but at a certain moment in life one is labelled aged or older (older than whom?) and life beyond that point is labelled aging'.[7] We are all, including gerontologists, aged and ageing; failing to recognise that age is situated on a continuum, rather than brusquely demarcated into distinct categories, we deprive ourselves of a framework for understanding the whole of our lives.

Still, one might ask with good reason, what can someone who is not old know or understand about what it means to be old? Is it possible for those who are not old to have insight into the lives of those who are? Literary critic Frank Kermode commented in a review he wrote in his late 80s:

Those who have had actual experience of old age are likely to be dead or very tired or just reluctant to discuss the matter with clever young interlocutors, so that much of the best thinking on this subject comes from philosophically sophisticated but honourably ignorant juniors.[8]

In response to a similar query, Margaret Gullette offers that 'Age is a field in which anyone who can do appropriate work in the right spirit has enough credentials'.[9] Age consciousness and age sensitivity (as directed towards oneself as well as others) is a vital criteria for any research—but this does not negate the importance of the life experience they bring to their scholarship. 'Honourably ignorant juniors' while pursuing their scholarship might well find they have much to learn.

Within gerontology, there have been a few notable exceptions to the general tendency to ignore the aging of the researcher.[10] Far from 'contaminating' the research, when gerontologists include their own experience of age as part of their analytic lens, their understanding about what they are documenting in others is richer and more nuanced. As Moody wrote more than 20 years ago: 'In recovering a human dimension in the study of aging, we will recover something important about ourselves. When we finally come to look into the "human face" of gerontology, we will understand at last that the face we see is simply our own'.[11] Jon Hendricks reflects 'turning the lantern light of inquiry onto one's self is a useful exercise...if our quest is to uncover new ground, it must be applicable first and foremost to us. If we cannot see ourselves in our explanations, perhaps we should pause before proffering them to the profession'.[12]

Gerontologist Martha Holstein's article 'On Being an Aging Woman', opens with the powerful proclamation of Grey Panthers founder Maggie Kuhn: 'I'm an old lady and damn proud of it'.[13] Holstein, in her 60s at the time of her writing, offers this observation about herself:

> I am very different at sixty-four than I was at forty-four and even fifty-four. Yes,
> there are continuities too...I know that I am not alone, and I should like to hear
> from my age peers about their experiences in growing older. If a strong sense
> that the personal is the political can be retrieved for aging women, then we have
> made a positive step.[14]

Holstein's statement here encapsulates the dynamic movement between continuity and change referred to by Bytheway earlier. Holstein continues, arguing '...at professional meetings, through writing both scholarly and personally, we have an obligation to speak to age as both material and constructed and to insist that the body is neither totally malleable nor totally determined'.[15] We need to reflect more actively not so much on the fact of our age, but on our individual and collective experiences of what age and aging mean in the context of our daily lives.

We look around us and gather up stories that help us to live our lives, help to see and understand a framework of meaning that may have eluded us had we not been exposed to these other stories. It is as if I am walking along a beach full of pebbles, and every so often the light reflects on one in a particular way, and I pause to collect it, and put it in my pocket. I continue on my walk, collecting up pebbles, and in the end, when I get home, I have a pocketful of these small multi-coloured objects, all shaped differently. These pebbles then join others which I have collected in other places and times—or maybe they were given to us by someone special, or remind us of a particular occasion. The pebbles are the stories which are available to us in our culture, through personal contacts, reading, and simply by living in and being part of our communities. I cannot collect all of the pebbles on the beach; I choose for myself those which for whatever small reason attract me: the water's shimmering reflection on it; the white line in the middle was in fact a circle around the whole, and this for me was a good-luck stone; or its near-heart shape made me smile. It is impossible to conceive of one's own story apart from those which one has heard from others. The pebbles are never really mine, but I collect them nonetheless. And bringing these particular pebbles together at this time is something which only I have done. They are not mine, but they are me.[16]

This passage comes from an article I wrote several years ago, in which I offered my views on contemporary models of successful aging. In this piece, I argued that throughout our lives, we interact with the world around us, observing people and places, affecting and being affected by our changing environment. I promoted the idea that as we travel, we should create for ourselves some kind of blueprint for our own old age. But such a project invariably raises questions: How can we ever know what we are going to become before we arrive there? How can we transform a wholly abstract exercise into something with flesh and bones? Where do we get the ingredients for building our blueprints?

Our lives are overspilling with such ingredients, if only we could see them. Some 'ingredients' might be identified in the negative, characteristics which one hopes not to adopt, not now, not ever. Writing in 1985, May argues that the increased longevity across the population introduces the question of people needing to 'learn how to age'. Critiquing what can be in some cases 'the long years of vapidity', he writes 'Just as the old should be convinced that whatever happens during senescence, they will never suffer exclusion, so they should understand that age does not exempt them from being despicable'.[17] May's article, though written in a deliberately provocative style, does direct one to the question of a moral responsibility to make our lives meaningful, for their duration. Rather than restricting our thoughts on aging to strategies of how we might avoid it, we should reconceptualise it as our journey of becoming, as we grow into ourselves.[18]

One of the key mechanisms for challenging the truncation of the human life cycle in to distinct stages is simply to talk to people. Talking to anyone about age—those who share our age, those who are younger, and those who are older—uncovers a lifespan framework which includes all of us. But candid conversations about age so rarely happen. Holstein addresses the importance of 'bringing older and younger women together to transform generational differences and expectations'.[19] The radical potential of inter-generational conversations for uncovering meaning in aging across the life cycle is still a relatively untapped resource.

In connection to an event I organised recently for International Women's Day, I had the occasion to invite my then 16-year-old daughter and some of her female friends to participate in a conversation about what it meant to them to be that age. Although I intuitively felt that they would have something to say about this, I was not wholly confident that they would be willing to talk about it with me, and in front of each other. In fact what transpired was very moving. They spent several hours talking and talking and talking about this topic. I had prepared a number of prompt questions, such as:

- Do you think your experience of being a 16-year-old girl is much differ- ent from that of your mum? How yes, how no?
- Looking to the future, if you had a daughter, what do you hope her expe- rience of being a girl will be like in comparison to yours? What would you hope would stay the same? What would you hope would be different?

In the beginning, the girls were somewhat reticent to speak, but as the time wore on, they became very animated. It was clear that they had a lot of things to say about this topic. What was most striking to me about this occasion, however, was that several of them later told me that no one had ever asked them questions like these. When one considers how much is taken for granted about the life worlds of our teenagers, it is striking how seldom we talk to them about how they feel being the age they are, and comparing this to the world they imagine that their parents grew up in, or that they envision for their own children.

Of course personal conversations are not the only encounter where one has the opportunity to listen to how people feel about their age. In the last quarter of the 20th century, oral history, with its emphasis on the spoken word, established itself as a subdiscipline of history. Those whose stories were being recorded gave first-hand accounts of history they had lived through, and often the speakers were reflecting back 50 years or longer. (This, in turn, has spurred a movement towards documenting memories in many communities.) American oral historian Studs Terkel, who died in 2008 at the age of 96, published a collection of interviews called *Coming of Age: The Story of our Century by Those Who've Lived It* which reached the *New York Times* bestseller list. Describing himself as 'an old battler paying tribute', Terkel completes his introduction with the following injunction:

> Think of what's stored in an eighty-, ninety-year-old mind. Just marvel at it. You see faces of people, places you've been to, images in your head. You've got a file nobody else has. *There'll be nobody like you ever again.* Make the most of every molecule you've got, as long as you've got a second to go. That's your charge.[20]

Although some of the individuals included in Terkel's book are famous, most are not. There is much food for thought contained in the nearly 500 pages.

There are other books which aim to collect the thoughts—often referred to as 'wisdom'—of old people: *8000 Years of Wisdom: 100 Octogenarians Share Their Lessons Learned from Life*[21] and *How to Live: A Search for Wisdom from Old People (While They Are Still on This Earth)*[22] are two examples. And there are special supplements in newspapers where, for one reason or another, the focus is on aging. I personally keep an ongoing file of interesting lives which I come across in newspapers or other forms of media. Thus it was that I encountered the likes of the artist and fly fisherman Bernard Venerables, who at the age of 93, describes himself as 'always working... very hard, seven days a week' and Betty Smith and Beryl Renwick, who at 90 and 86, respectively, are the oldest people ever to have won a Gold at the Sony Awards. My personal favorite is Mamy Rock, who, as a 70-year-old DJ who lights up dance floors across Europe, gives new meaning to the term 'aging rock n' roller' (a description I would readily apply to myself). Looking straight in to the cameras, with her spiked grey hair and bright red lipstick, she tells her fans 'Keep rockin'. When I grow up, I want to be like her.

Sometimes the media focuses on one particular old person who is remarkable. Two examples of these are Harry Patch and Jeanne Clement. In 2008, then Poet Laureate Andrew Motion was commissioned to write a poem for the oldest surviving veteran of World War I, 109-year-old Harry Patch. Motion describes feeling 'a heavy burden... to pay Mr. Patch due respect, to celebrate him and honour him, but at the same time not to let those feelings of something approaching awe get in the way of having a normal conversation'. He then elaborates on a moment in their meeting:

> Before we said goodbye, Harry breathed me a joke: he thought that because he'd been alive for such a long time, he might as well go on for ever. What he meant, in all modest seriousness, was that he knew his own value as one of the very few who are still able to say, "The war was like this; I was there." This, in turn, means that he is also one of the very few whose eyes we can look into and imagine we see what they saw, whose hands we can hold and feel they are leading us back through time. To sit in his company is to feel the flow between "then" and "now" is unbroken.[23]

That November was the last Remembrance Sunday that Harry Patch would see; he died a few months later—the oldest man in Europe, and the last remaining British male to have been born in the 19th century.

Although Jeanne Calment did not see the battlefields of the World War I, she did see with her own eyes Vincent Van Gogh who resided in her hometown of Arles. (She was not very impressed with his demeanor.) Clement, who died in 1997, lived until the age of 122. The French attributed her longevity to the fact that 'she used to eat more than two pounds of chocolate a week and treat her skin with olive oil, rode a bicycle until she was 100, and only quit smoking five years ago'. At the end of an interview when she was 117, the interviewer left her, saying 'Until next year, perhaps', to which she retorted: 'I don't see why not! You don't look so bad to me'. The Mayor of Arles, where she lived, described her as 'the living memory of our city'.[24]

In the context of the present discussion, what is outstanding about both Patch and Calment's lives is that they lasted such a long time. Whether longevity in and of itself is something which is to be desired is something for individuals to decide for themselves[25]; however, in both of these cases, it is not only the number of years lived, but indeed the role of being a 'living memory', the embodiment of history, connecting the present to an earlier time that sets these lives apart from others.

In the university classes I teach on aging, I begin by asking students to write about old people who are in their lives: What are they like, what are their relationships like with them, what is their appearance, how do they spend their time? When I began teaching the class, I anticipated that my students would produce mostly negative descriptions of the old people in their lives. In fact the reverse has been the case. Although there are some very bleak pictures which have been painted over the years, what I have learned is that many of our students have significant relationships with older people, who they respect and who they would like to emulate in terms of learning how to age. Although they do not often talk about this with their peers, for many of them, they do not need to look very far at all to find inspiration for their blueprints for aging. However, in most cases, these older people are family members.[26] Furman opens her book, an ethnographic study of a hair salon in the United States, with the statement: 'Few of us get to interact in a meaningful way with older people who are unrelated to us; as a consequence, until recently I knew little about old age'.[27] Although we can learn a lot from the old people in our daily lives, we are not limited to our private worlds when we go in search of those who can teach us about living meaningful, long lives.

It is not unusual for people to be able to identify mentors for aging, people who they admire and from whom they think they have much to learn. When gerontologist Robert Butler, who founded the U.S. National Institute on Aging and who was the person who first coined the term 'ageism', was asked about influences which helped to shape him, he said it was his grandmother who had taught him about the will to survive. (His book *Why Survive? Being Old in America* was awarded the Pulitzer Prize). Orphaned at a young age, Butler went to live with his grandparents on their farm, which they eventually lost in the Depression. His grandfather died, and he and his grandmother moved into a hotel, which burned down, with all their possessions. 'What I remember even more than the hardships of those years was my grandmother's triumphant spirit and determination', he wrote. 'Experiencing at first hand an older person's struggle to survive, I was myself helped to survive as well'.[28] When Butler himself died in 2010, the range of obituaries around the world were a testament to the role he had played in the lives of others. From a tribute printed in *The Hindu*, he is remembered as

> the epitome of aging with dignity, grace and good health, a role model for younger gerontologists like me... He was a practitioner of all that he prescribed. His sharpness, alertness and vitality till he died is exemplary....His energy, enthusiasm for work, ability to share was infectious.[29]

A mentor for aging, indeed. Butler with his insight into aging, Jeanne Calment and her weekly two pounds of chocolate, Studs Terkel and those like him whose lives spanned most of the 20th century, Harry Patch and his memories of the trenches, and of course Mamy Rock who discovered a new calling for herself when she listened to the music of her grandson—all of these people and countless others help us to imagine our future lives, even while we accept that we cannot determine our fate.

CREATIVITY AND AGING

Paradox, by Vera Newsom

Must I be peaceful in old age, add to the tapestry
a few lazy stitches, self still ravenous?
A hawk hovers and my spirit soars,
swoops on once vital nerve and sinew, turns
cannibal. What else can I devour
but my own resinous heart?
The young are too young to understand desire,
to savour wild strawberries or comprehend
the precise artistry of feet that dance
on the precipice edge. Barefoot they dance
who have no knowledge of frayed ligaments
or the eye that cannot bear the depth of height.
Now only, when breath comes short, can we assess
the clarity of air The burn-out season
denies, and evokes, the sharp green of new shoots
and the dried creek recalls the overflow of rain.
Young, we love, grasp, consume. Old, we savour.
And the taste sends us wild.[30]

The paradox which forms the title of this poem is indeed the very point of contention in discussions on the role of creativity in later life—a topic which has interested people through the ages.

In the last decade, the question of the nature of creativity in old age has been taken up by Edward Said, who, builds on Theodore Adorno's concept of 'late style', first articulated in Spätstil Beethovens' (1937). In the introduction to *Late Style,* Said's book on the subject which was posthumously published, Michael Wood describes the meaning of the term 'late' in his introduction:

> ... death does sometimes wait for us, and it is possible to become deeply aware of its waiting. The quality of time alters then, like a change in the light, because the present is so thoroughly shadowed by other seasons: the revived or receding past, the newly unmeasurable future; the unimaginable time beyond time. With such moments we arrive at the conditions for the special sense of lateness that is the subject of this book.[31]

Is there some marked quality which affects the character of creativity in old age? Said argues that although there are many examples which one can identify in which the final years of an artist's life 'crown a lifetime of aesthetic endeavour'—and here he supplies names such as Rembrandt and Matisse, Bach and Wagner—he is in fact more interested in cases of artists for whom their craft in late life communicates 'not as harmony and resolution, but as intransigence, difficulty and contradiction. What if age and ill health don't produce serenity at all'? he asks. 'Far from resolution', Said is drawn to works which 'suggest an angry and disturbed artist who uses [in the case of Ibsen] drama as an occasion to stir up more anxiety, tamper irrevocably with the possibility of closure, leave the audience more perplexed and unsettled than before'—something which Said characterizes as 'deliberately unproductive productiveness, a going against'.[32]

Like Adorno, Said uses the late work of Ludgwig Beethoven to illustrate his argument. Beethovan's late works, he argues, constitute nothing less than

> ...an event in the history of modern culture: a moment when the artist who is fully in command of his medium nevertheless abandons communication with the established social order of which he is a part and achieves a contradictory, alienated relationship with it.[33]

Adorno, who refers to Beethoven as 'lonely prince of a realm of spirits' remarks on the 'fractured' nature of the late works, whose maturity 'does not resemble the kind one finds in fruit. They are...not round, but furrowed, even ravaged. Devoid of sweetness, bitter and spiny, they do not surrender themselves to mere delectation'. Said, quoting Adorno, says 'Beethoven does not bring about a "harmonious synthesis"', but tears them apart in time, in order, perhaps, to preserve them for the eternal'. What Said is arguing is that late style, by refusing to conform to expectations of inner calm, can, in fact, be marked by real genius. Many of the examples he uses are of people whose final works, while breaking with their earlier style, in fact foreshadow future developments in the arts. Said, who wrote the essays at the end of his life and proclaims the topic to 'interest me for obvious personal reasons' leaves no doubt that there is much to recommend 'going against the grain' but it is not an easy path. When Said's On Late Style was published posthumously, it was praised by Hanif Kureshi as 'An exercise in late style itself, full of melancholy, insight and humour'.[34]

Whether or not 'late style' can be used to describe the work of many, or even most, artists in late life is not something which I will take up here. For every example one can point to of a turbulent 'going against', one can find others who discover an inner peace, for whom the final years represent a time of coming to terms with oneself and one's life. 'In the country of old age the natives are as different from one another as anywhere else'.[35]

In contrast to the 'late style' described by Adorno and Said, some artists do indeed find deep within themselves a new sense of balance, even peace. Bharatanatyam dance artist Chitra Sundaram identifies a new level of authenticity she finds that age brings to dance.

> Indian dance, was, and is about love. And as we grow older, our notion, our understanding, our experience of it, and how comfortable we are with love and all things commonly associated with love—youth, beauty, passion—changes…not becomes less or more, but changes. It changes, anxious to remain authentic, truthful to itself.…Dancemakers, especially as they mature, are exquisitely vulnerable to this unbearable heaviness of being, and it shows in their work…It also reaches for places in our souls, when physical virtuosity is done amazing us.[36]

I had the delight in witnessing this first hand, when I was invited to participate in an event called Time to Move: A National Conference Celebrating Older People Dancing. (Fortunately I was invited as a speaker, though I did have a chance to display my two left feet when I enlisted in the workshop led by the inspiring performer and choreographer Bisakha Sarker). At the conference, I saw not only professional older dancers from around the UK, but also became acquainted with the widespread use of dance as a way of bringing together older people in the community, as well as being used as a vehicle for working with specific bodily ailments, such as Parkinson's. For some people, at least, it was clear that the increased physical limitations that come with later life were also accompanied by an uncovering of new layers of creativity.

The last quarter of a century has seen a significant rise in fiction writing by and about older people, with the increased number of older people in the population. Paraphrasing Canadian gerontologist Constance Rooke, writers and readers are 'eager to explore what it [feels] like to be old'.[37] Unlike some forms of creativity which demand quick memory recall or physical dexterity, writing and reading seem to be capabilities which benefit from time, experience, psychological complexity, and an inclination towards reflection, and thus it is not surprising that some people only begin to write in their later years, and some of those who have been writing for decades find a voice with a new maturity. Within the field of gerontology, there has been growing attention paid to stories of aging,[38] because 'writing and reading stories can make [a contribution] to the issue of making sense of the differences between the perspectives of insiders and outsiders on ageing and death'.[39] Wyatt-Brown summarizes the lure to fiction for both older writers and readers:

> Authors are just as vulnerable to physical decline and the loss of important people in their lives as are the rest of us. Being able to write about disability, loss,

and mourning, however allows them to share the experiences with a wide audience. Readers can take comfort in the knowledge that others have experienced the struggles that feel so threatening, painful, and never-ending.[40]

But not all fiction with old people as main characters is about loss and suffering. Gabriel Garcia Marquez's *Love in the Time of Cholera* is hard to beat in the romantic sweepstakes; the book opens with a scene after a period of 'fifty-one years, nine months, and four days', when Florentino is finally able to tell his beloved Femina (who stands at her husband's grave) 'I have waited for this opportunity for more than half a century, to repeat to you once again my vow of eternal fidelity and everlasting love'.[41] From here they fall in, and out, and in love again. Crazy kids.

The final domain of creativity I shall just mention here is that of gardening, or what Cicero referred to as 'the pleasures of agriculture'. Mark Bhatti (2006) has explored the role of gardening in later years, describing gardens as 'a key site for ageing' as well as 'a site of resistance to ageing'.[42] He concludes that 'gardens are an important part of older people's sense of home, and gardening as a form of bodily action and power is significant in home making'.[43]

Gardening is a hobby for which I have neither aptitude nor inclination. Yet I cannot ignore that for many people, of many ages, this activity is not only enjoyable but serves as a metaphor for the process of human aging. Cicero, in *De Senectute* clarifies that 'it is not the revenue which charms me, but the very nature and properties of the soil'. He then confides to his reader

> ...the secret of what gives my old age repose and amusement. I pass over the inherent power of things generated from the earth, which, from so tiny a grape or fig seed, or from the minute seeds of other fruits and plants, produces such massive trunks and shoots, sprouts, cuttings, divisions, and layers enough to afford wonder and delight to any man.[44]

Cicero's documenting of this delight is marked by both its length and enthusiasm. But he is not alone. Germaine Greer offers a more contemporary explanation, but here Cicero is never far away.

> Gardening is all in the future, and the less future people have, the more they tend to think about it. Gardeners are never satisfied with what's in front of them; they are always planting, rooting up, building and then knocking down, but as they grow older, they spend more time standing and staring...Everyone loves that well which he must leave ere long.[45]

Figure 3.1:
Scottish miner and lifetime communist Andrew Clark is an example of someone who, in his old age, has derived much pleasure from the cultivation of a beautiful garden.

The historian Roy Strong offers an explicit theory of the connection of human aging and gardening.

> Gardening is an expression of maturity, because you have grown yourself to understand how other things grow. [Gardening] is a mutant art form that could be paralleled with painting. All the great painters—Titan, Rembrandt—got better in old age.... the same happens with gardening; you understand more what you want.... The garden has always been a mirror of the cycle of life into death, followed by the resurrection of spring. It is an allegory of both the beauty and tragedy of human life.[46]

Gardens can be a site of great imagination, creativity, and where many hours of everyday lives are lived out, physically and psychologically.[47] As we see from these passages, it is the conjoining of physical activity with the metaphor of growth, decline and renewal which is particularly compelling for some people who choose to garden in late life.

In this section, I have considered a wide array of creative pursuits in old age—musicians, playwrights, dancers, literary theorists, novelists, gardeners and more. Although creativity demands an engagement of the mind, indeed of the imagination, more often than not, it also involves the body. (Painter Pip Benveniste wrote to me while in her 80s: 'I am so lucky that my life has not worn out my imagination—only my lungs'). But we and our bodies cannot be fully separated. Anyone who doubts this need only read historian Tony Judt's harrowing essay 'Night' in which he describes trying to 'divert my mind from the body in which it is encased. The pleasures of mental agility are much overstated, inevitably—as it now appears to me— by those not exclusively dependent upon them'.[48]

BODIES

Music composer John Cage reflects on how later life gave him a new appreciation for the importance of his body.

> ...I now see that the body is part and parcel of the whole being. There isn't a split between the mind and the body; they both belong together. When I was younger, I mistreated the body because I thought the mind was what I was really dealing with. But as I get older I see that I'm dealing quite straightforwardly with the body and that I must keep it in good working order as long as I can.[49]

Cage's statement that he mistreated his younger body 'because I thought the mind was what I was really dealing with' resonates with the experience of many others. Even those who have not led lives which are particularly physically active might find in the aging process a new appreciation for their bodies.

I had my first taste of this in my early 30s. A sledding accident landed me with a broken hip in a French hospital, where—with one exception— the other patients were about 50 years older than me. Through experiencing agonizing pain for weeks, and chronic discomfort for months, I gained access to an embodied knowledge that I would have never known had it not been for my accident. I felt as if all I had written on the topic of meaning making in old age was from an angle of blissful ignorance. (It was not that I was unaware of the impact of physical challenges to the aging body, but I always somehow found it to look beyond these. From my hospital bed, the view beyond my body did not extend very far). As I slowly recovered from my injury, so, too, I regained confidence that there was at least some value in the work I was doing. But one insight that has stayed with me in the interim of two decades is that it is very difficult to imagine embodiment and its limitations. Even when we think we can 'rise above' the purely physical, we are reminded that without our bodies we are nothing. We need them to work, and when they begin to break down and malfunction—an inevitable part of aging—our sense of who we are is also challenged.

If few gerontologists write about their own aging, even fewer talk about their aging bodies. One notable exception is Martha Holstein, who writes of the 'strangeness' of occupying a mid-60s body, and her 'uneasiness with what my body is becoming'. Here she elaborates:

> That uneasiness, I think, has two sources. For one, it derives from how I imagine I am perceived in relation to other, younger bodies and, indeed, to my own midlife body. I assume that people... may draw conclusions about me by looking at my body. I am still objectified but now not in terms of sexual desirability but rather as one without importance sexual or otherwise... second, my uneasiness emerges from my recognition that each day, this body, my most immediate contact with the world, is edging closer to death. I am day by day more vulnerable.[50]

It is not just that we have to reach a new understanding about our body—what it can and can't do, and how, in turn, that affects my self-perception of what kind of a person I am—but our bodies are changing; they are in a perpetual process of becoming. So our present embodied selves are not only different from what they once were, but they are also different from what they will be. And here the imagination is a critical tool, helping us to construct the selves of both past and future. In chapter 2 I recounted how I used to climb the trees across the street from my home. Was I ever such a tree climber in reality as I have come to construct my childhood self in my memory? What is for sure is that I am no tree climber now. And yet, I have no doubt that I will not always be able to count on many physical pursuits which I take for granted in my daily life—long walks in the Lake District, rowing with various members of my family, the thrill of jumping big waves, long swims on Lake Erie, these things and many, many more which provide a simple but deep source of happiness.

Holstein remarks that 'Cultural messages support the denial of change; by implying that age should be no more than an artefact, we hear the message that we need be no different in old age than we were in middle age... as if our very visible bodies can be simply denied away'.[51] The tendency towards denying difference is reminiscent of Ndlovu's observation in the previous chapter, regarding the attitudes of those who would happily pretend that they don't 'see' his black skin, despite the very real impact that 'race' exercises on people's lives. Implicitly, and sometimes explicitly, we are instructed that the best way to fight ageism (or racism) is to act as if these differences were not there—in other words, to deny our own lived realities. And yet for Holstein, even while she acknowledges the cultural subterfuge, the message of denial is internalised: 'I have not yet been able to look at myself in the mirror or imaginatively see myself through

Figure 3.2:
Peace activist Eileen Daffern, who died a few days after her 98th birthday.

the eyes of those much younger than myself and feel assertively proud and powerful'.[52]

Holstein's experience differs from that of Eileen Daffern. Writing in her late 80s, she cautions:

> Taking pride in one's appearance should not disappear with old age. When my mother was 90, I used to catch her looking at herself in the large Victorian mirror in my living room as she was dressing to go out. Her gestures were those of a young girl preening herself. Such a strong image of self gave me a positive picture of ageing and I, too, look in the mirror.[53]

Indeed, till the day she died, at the age of 98, Eileen was always very well turned out, someone who could carry off wearing hats, scarves, and interesting jewellery with little apparent self-consciousness, exhibiting a sense of style which was both comfortable but considered. With her white hair (always in a lose bun) and her energetic gesticulations, she offered a healthy antidote to the cultural erasure of old bodies.

May[54] argued that bodies have a 'three-fold meaning' for human beings: '(1) as an instrument for controlling the world, that is, 'hands for working, feet for walking, tongue for talking'; (2) as a means of savoring the world, via our five senses; and (3) as a means of revealing ourselves to others: We not only *have* bodies, we *are* our bodies'.[55] Each of these dimensions of meaning are affected not only in our old age, but throughout our lives, as we come to have new (sometimes more, sometimes less) capabilities; as our senses—and our appreciation of them—develop and then recede; and finally as our means for being in the world. Without our bodies, we are no longer. What Holstein's earlier statement reflects is that we not only come to know ourselves differently—our bodily changes do mean something—but that, like Holstein, we imagine how others see us as well. Watching those around us, and watching them watching us, is the way many come to experience their own aging. Eileen Daffern reflects on this process of mirroring:

It is through others as in a mirror that I realise my age—in the wrinkles of an old friend not seen for a long time, in the shock of realising that my children are into middle age, or in the consideration that I get from the stranger who gets up to give me a seat in a packed bus or train.[56]

Holstein comments that her aging body tells her she is 'edging her way closer to death'. This requires the ultimate leap of imagination, to see in my mind's eye a world in which I am no longer there; every character someone else, but nowhere am I. The realisation that one is reaching the end of one's story prompts many people to ask themselves fundamental question about the meaning of the lives they have lived.

'TAKING HOLD OF EXPERIENCE'

The last of Erik Erikson's eight identity crises which demarcate different stages, or hurdles, of development, is the challenge to the individual to accept 'one's own and only life...an acceptance of the fact that one's life is one's own responsibility'.[57] The balancing act between 'ego integrity' and 'despair' which Erikson identifies as life's final challenge, resonates with the experience of many as they try to make sense of their lives. This coming to terms involves the individual in reviewing their past, revisiting key events, relationships, sources of joy and disappointment, and potentially gaining new insight into their role in determining the direction of their lives.

This process of re-evaluation has much in common with life review, the term used by gerontologist Robert Butler to describe

a naturally occurring, universal mental process characterized by the progressive return to consciousness of past experiences, and, particularly, the resurgence of unresolved conflicts; simultaneously, and normally, these revived experiences and conflicts can be surveyed and reintegrated. Presumably this process is prompted by the realization of approaching dissolution and death...[58]

Like Erikson, Butler believed that as persons neared the end of their lives, they were compelled to revisit their pasts, and to come to terms with the lives they had lived. Life review in this sense is not mere reminiscence (though it will include it), but involves the more rigorous task of taking stock.

Perhaps one of the most important tasks of aging is that of re-imagining time, in its different registers. Even while one becomes aware that the time remaining for one's own self is diminishing, there is a deepening appreciation for the on-going nature of life itself. Randall (2013) argues that the aging process pushes us 'toward a more ironic stance... marked by increased acceptance of uncertainty and ambiguity'[59] Being ironic, Randall explains,

is to have a certain distance on things, to view them critically or from the 'edge'... to be ironic is to be mindful of the numerous perspectives from which all phenomena can be interpreted, the multiple narratives that we can spin around them, and the indeterminacy of meaning that's thus implied.[60]

This ironic stance is 'more flexible, more expansive, and more accepting of uncertainty,' and it is intricately bound up with the act of narrative reflection, or life review. Narrative reflection plays a 'pivotal role in the development of self-understanding'[61] as we continually are 'looking back over the terrain of the past from the standpoint of the present and either seeing things anew or drawing "connections"...that could not possibly be drawn during the course of on-going moments but only in retrospect'.[62] With increased age, we come to appreciate that the meaning which we give to our experiences is only one possible way of understanding the lives we have lived; this, in turn, brings an enhanced awareness of 'the lives we haven't lived'.[63]

An appreciation of the passing of time, and of the temporary nature of our own existence, has the potential to instil in us a greater tolerance for ambiguity, and ultimately, for the transient nature of life itself.[64] Although the confrontation with 'temporal limitation' is, for some, a source of much disquietude, for Freud the reverse is true: 'Limitation in the possibility of an enjoyment raises the value of the enjoyment...A flower that blossoms only for a single night does not seem to us on that account less lovely'.[65] That our days are measured is thus not something to be regretted, but rather invites us to treat with care the time which we have been allocated.

Eileen Daffern comments in her autobiography that

Growing older brings with it both an obsession with and a changed perception of time...With age, the present continues to be all-important, and more consciously so because there is still so much to do. Time is accelerated, and in a way it becomes our adversary... I am increasingly aware of the here and now, and the need to savour each moment.[66]

However, it is not that the older person is living in the past for the sake of the past, but rather revisiting the past in light of present, the future which had (previously) yet to unfold. Eileen Daffern quotes a passage from *Mrs. Dalloway*, in which a character reflects on growing old: 'The passions remain as strong, but one has gained—at last—the power which adds the supreme flavor to existence—the power of taking hold of experience, of turning it around slowly in the light'.[67] Daffern ruminates on what this 'turning over' has meant for her personally, describing it as 'one of the greatest benefits of old age. Memory, by letting me re-live times past and discover lost time, has helped me to give shape to all my experiences: a rounding off, as it were, of life'.[68] Despite the predominance of the past as it reappears in the present, thoughts for the future are never far away. With increased age and a sense of one's own limited time remaining, the sense of the future is altered, sometimes resulting in an enhanced concern for the world which one will leave behind.

This examining, and re-examining of one's life experiences is not something which is necessarily restricted to late life. In the 50-plus years since Butler published his original work on life review, many scholars have followed Butler's lead in associating this process with the end of life, but there are other moments in our lives which can cause us to stop in our tracks and review where we have come from and where we are going.[69] Although these deep self-reflections are usually associated with traumatic events, such as the loss of loved ones, serious illness, or living through acute political change, it is also possible to consciously engage in such scrutiny in our everyday lives, asking ourselves what is the life we will want to look back on? If we use our imaginations to look forward in order to imagine looking backwards, we increase the likelihood that our ultimate life review will bring us some level of satisfaction. (Here the question of narrative imagination enters with a particular force of purpose.) This is something I have always tried to ingrain into my children. This summer I received some of my own medicine, when my daughter tried to persuade me to go skinny dipping with her on a beautiful warm night. 'What is it that you will want to look back on? Getting an extra hour's sleep, or going swimming'? she asked. The swim was exquisite.

Reflexive time travelling, revisiting the past in light of the present or ruminating on a hoped for future, invariably involves imagining ourselves somewhere. Our sense of place, throughout our lives, is an important part of the stories we live, remember and recreate. Twenty-five years ago, when I first interviewed Eileen Daffern for a project I was conducting on lifetime socialist activists, she began by showing me photos of the Yorkshire mill village on the edge of the moors, where she had grown up as a child. 'All that you know about *Wuthering Heights*, that's where I walked in my childhood. Laid upon the hills... I think that has bitten very deep into me' she told me. Years later, she settled in Brighton, where she lived in the same house for 40 years. In her autobiography, she asks 'Why do people uproot in old age, I wonder? It adds to loneliness'.[70] Our sense of place and of belonging are often intricately bound, and if one becomes physically dislocated, a feeling of alienation is often not far behind. Our roots need to be nourished.

Kevin McHugh evokes the importance of place:

> Place is the first and last of all things. Our entrance to, and exit from, this earthly realm is 'place-ful'... We enjoin and constitute place collectively, slipping and sliding into the future, generations unfolding, overlapping and pushing forward as a fugue... the press of everyday life and practice is scarcely noticed as the very creation and re-creation of place; we swim in place like fish in the sea. Only after the fact, when we stop and reflect, might we (re)call our lives as a journey in and through place, so that we 'see' place as shifting sand bars in a coursing stream.[71]

For some, it is the deep sense of enduring place which makes their own limited time on earth more acceptable. Even after we depart, we know that the places that have been the backdrop for all that we have done in our lives, will continue to exist.

CONTEMPLATING FINITUDE

Cicero concludes *De Senectute* by affirming that 'nature imposes a limit upon life as upon all else'.[72] And yet, though we might know and understand the universal fact of death, translating this from an 'objective matter to a personal one',[73] demands that we contemplate our own nonexistence. Jean Améry tells us '...the fact of my death...is only comprehensible for the survivors and only by them to be integrated into the course of affairs'.[74] And yet it is the very end of my story, my death, which seals the completion of my life. Ironically we will never live to see the finale which belongs most profoundly to us. Améry describes death as 'the future of all futures. Every step we take leads us to it, every thought we think breaks down on it'.[75] And though we all know that eventually our lives will end, this knowledge has a different implication for those who are old.

Though all of us will die one day, those who are lucky enough to make it to an old age know that the road ahead is not long. Though death is often

597.—Antique Bust of Cicero.

Figure 3.3:
Cicero's *De Senectute* was written in 44 AD and still has relevance to today's world.

associated with old age, of all those who are alive, it is they who have managed longest not to die. Still, we are all of us mortal. As poet Philip Larkin reminds us, for those who manage to make it to old age

The peak that stays in view wherever we go
For them is *rising ground*[76]

Cicero argues that being old and knowing that the future is not long is not in itself reason for remorse.

Nature struggles and rebels when the young die. When they die it is as if a violent fire is extinguished by a torrent, but the old die like a spent fire quenched of its own accord and without external effort. Unripe apples must be wrenched from the tree, but fall of their own accord when ripe and mellow; so from the young it is force that takes life, from the old, ripeness.[77]

Although some people suffer terribly from a deep-seated fear surrounding the fact of their mortality, this isn't always the case. Robert Butler, in his mid-80s, reported 'I feel less threatened by the end of life than I perhaps did when I was 35',[78] an example perhaps of the 'ripeness'—a long and full life—described by Cicero. At the heart of what Cicero writes is the idea that a good death comes with a certain timeliness. We all can recognize the 'violent fire' that attends the mourning of one who has died young. But what of those deaths which come too late, after much suffering and where the physical body exists as an encasement for a person who is no longer there? Frank Kermode describes the death of Job, who dies 'being old and full of days':

> To die thus at just the right moment depends, in life, not on narrative logic but on what Bernard Williams calls 'moral luck'. It is what enables a person to die when full of days, old but not in terminal misery, correctly mourned by a numerous and prosperous family. It is not an ending one can choose, it is a matter of aesthetics.[79]

As medical doctor Sherwin Nuland writes 'Death rarely, if ever, acts according to our plans or even to our expectations'.[80] None of us know what will be the circumstances which will lead to our death—all we know is that we will die. And it is this knowledge which ultimately lends meaning to our lives. Our sense of our own mortality is what makes us human. In *Humbolt's Gift*, Saul Bellow refers to death as 'the dark backing that a mirror needs if we are to see anything'. We need finitude in order that our lives might have purpose, and the knowledge of finitude frames the whole of our lives. The fact that life ends 'makes more precious each hour of those we have been given: it demands that life must be useful and rewarding'.[81].

And so, like Freddie Mercury, we might ask 'Who wants to live forever'? Yet the nearing of our own final hour can be hard to accept, even terrifying for some. As Améry writes, even those who accept the immanence of their death, when they see the 'Executioner' plead 'not tonight, just not at this hour. Every night is tonight and every hour is this hour, and every time an appeal is made to the court'.[82]

But what lies at the heart of this appeal? Clara, one of the participants in Frida Furman's study *Facing the Mirror*, explains 'The greatest trauma of growing old...is the fact that we leave this world and all the people in it, all the loved ones. This, I think, is the most traumatic. Not so much the dying as the leaving. The leaving. The separation.'[83]

If living, and aging, are marked by our relationships with those around us, then contemplating our deaths means contemplating a severance of those relationships. And it is this that causes for many not so much a crisis of the imagination, but of the heart. We want to be with our children all their lives, to be a source of refuge for them, come what may. And yet for most of us, this will not happen (and nor would it be satisfactory for us to outlive our children[84]). Although it might be that even after we are gone memories of us may linger in the lives of those whom we once knew, the fact remains that we will be separated. And it will be up to those who we leave behind to carry on with the project of living, until it is their turn to depart. One could say here that moral philosophy and evolution are intertwined. As Nuland explains:

> We die so that the world may continue to live. We have been given the miracle of life because trillions and trillions of living things have prepared the way for us and then have died—in a sense, for us. We die, in turn, so that others may live. The tragedy of a single individual becomes, in the balance of natural things, the triumph of ongoing life.[85]

This sense of an ongoing future of a world in which we have (already) played our part is for some, at least, a source of comfort. But this requires great imagination.

John Moat writes: '...as I grow old and mystery seems somehow more immediate, I find a quickening sense not only of my life being something imagined, but as being individually party to the Imagining; and—just as everyone else's unique life is—essential to its completeness'.[86] Age brings with it the opportunity for new kinds of imaginings. The lives we have lived are also the lives we have imagined, even though they may not always be the lives we once imagined they might have been.

CHAPTER 4

Education

Walking along the river one day, my teenage son turned and asked me if I could have any job in the world, what would I choose. He is someone who always stretches the limits of the possible, and as such, my response did not need to be restricted to any particular historical period. We walked along the path in silence for a few moments, as I contemplated the enormity of the question. Although I wanted to be worthy of this Grand Question, I could not help but feel that the answer was simple. I would choose the job I have: a teacher and a scholar.

I am intrigued by how we come to claim expert knowledge about education. Several years ago I was invited to be a keynote speaker at a conference organized by the Canadian Ministry of Education. Although flattered, initially I was reluctant to accept the invitation. I was not, I explained, an education specialist. The person who invited me simply responded by saying that she was aware that I had been teaching for several decades. Was this really not something I felt I knew something about? Since that time I have reflected on my initial reaction. Why did I not feel that my experiential knowledge 'counted'?

The discourse of 'imagination' is often employed in relation to the establishment and evaluation of educational goals and standards—with little apparent agreement amongst the many voices. It is probably not necessary, nor even possible, to reconcile those viewpoints. Rather, in this chapter, I will use my experience as someone who has taught students with an age range of 60 years on both sides of the Atlantic as a lens for exploring the potential for our classrooms to be, in the words of bell hooks 'locations(s) of possibility.'[1]

THE FEELING OF INFINITY

Mary Warnock has devoted attention to the study of imagination, examining both its importance as a concept within philosophy, and the ways in which it is practically facilitated or blocked in the public domain, particularly in the realm of education. As someone who has played a number of roles within a wide range of educational settings, she knows the vital importance of tapping into the imagination in the complex and interwoven processes of teaching and learning. She writes:

> The belief that there is more in our experience of the world than can possibly meet the unreflecting eye, that our experience is significant for us, and worth the attempt to understand it... this kind of belief may be referred to as the feeling of infinity. It is a sense... that there is always *more* to experience, and *more in* what we experience than we can predict. Without some such sense, even at the quite human level of there being something which deeply absorbs our interest, human life becomes perhaps not actually futile or pointless, but experienced as if it were. It becomes, that is to say, boring.... it is the main purpose of education to give people the opportunity of never ever being, in this sense, bored: or not ever succumbing to a feeling of futility, or to the belief that they have come to an end of what is worth having... if education has a justification, this salvation for those who... need it must be its justification.[2]

Igniting imagination is, then, the purpose of education, as this provides the impetus to explore what lies beyond known experience. The issues which Warnock eloquently identifies here are indeed some of the major challenges which confront those of us who teach. How do we effectively communicate to our students that what they experience in their own worlds is important and even significant, but that, at the same time, the world extends far beyond this? Often, it is challenge enough to demonstrate to our students that what we wish to teach them has relevance to their own lives. But we must be able to take them further than that, to show them 'that there is always more to experience, and more in what we experience than we can predict'. If we can even begin to demonstrate to students that there are important connections between their individual lives and the world of ideas—in other words to make them thirsty for a sense of what lies beyond—then we have done much.

Warnock refers to the aim of 'imaginative understanding'.[3] This requires us both to make connections between things, to synthesize, as well as to throw that which seems of a whole into chaotic disarray. Warnock identifies different levels at which the imagination is employed:

> If... our imagination is at work tidying up the chaos of sense experience, at a different level it may, as it were, untidy it again. It may suggest that there are vast unexplored areas, huge spaces of which we may get only an occasional awe-inspiring glimpse, questions raised by experience about whose answers we can only with hesitation speculate.[4]

It is our imagination which pushes us to see beyond what already is appar-ent, either experientially or perceptually. And as Warnock indicates, it is this 'looking beyond' which has the potential to spark the curiosity of stu-dents, to lift them from 'boredom.' Paradoxically, through the exercise of our imagination, we can begin to perceive alliances and contradictions that were previously hidden from our view. In this sense, one can see the basis of an argument that a multi- and particularly interdisciplinary approach to teaching (and research) creates an atmosphere which is fertile for the imagination.

It is through our imagination that we not only come to know other worlds, but indeed ourselves, and the way this is expressed is in our on-going narration of our lives. According to Moat (2012b)

> ... there is an existential onus on each individual 'to know thyself'—to tell his or her own story... The full of this can be achieved only through recourse to the Imagination: to provide guidance and opportunity for this to happen must, one would have thought, be the primary concern of genuine education... [when] the individual is cut off from the Imagination... his or her story is suspended.[5]

Knowing ourselves, as selves in whom change and constancy are intricately enmeshed, is a project without end, as was discussed in the last chapter. This ongoing narration of the self is only possible through the use of our imagination, as our sense of our identity is a fundamental negotiation between what exists, and what does not exist (but might yet, or might have done so in the past). If we cannot visualise other possible ways of being, then our story becomes 'suspended'.

Samuel Coleridge argued that it is the imagination which brings into balance opposite or discordant qualities. Building on this precept, Peter Murphy elaborates:

> ... creative acts are formed of elements which are borrowed from widely sepa-rated domains. That is why disciplinary drudges, even highly published ones, who plough the same field continuously, produce little or nothing of inter-est. The imagination borrows things from the most unlikely sources and compounds them.[6]

However, even though imagination inclines us towards synthesis, the same ability to re-conceptualise what holds things together can also serve to break down what had seemed whole. Imagination is not innocent, fuzzy and warm. Imaginative understanding can lead us to question the very founda-tions on which we have built order in our lives. Thus it is that we use our imagination to detach ourselves from what is familiar, giving us a new perception of not only what is there, but also what is absent. Warnock, elaborating on the views of Sartre, writes about the crucial relationship between presence and absence in the creative functioning of the imagination:

> ... there is a power in the human mind which is at work in our everyday perception of the world, and is also at work in our thought about what is absent; which enables us to see the world, whether present or absent as significant, and also to present this vision to others, for them to share or reject. And this power, though it gives us 'thought-imbued' perception... is not only intellectual. Its impetus comes from the emotion as much as from the reason, from the heart as much as from the head.[7]

So what can we as educators do to stimulate this 'thought-imbued perception'? How can we encourage our students to think meaningfully about their experiences, to gain a deeper understanding not only of their individual lives but of their wider social contexts, and further, to move beyond that known world? What can we do as teachers so that our students can experience 'the feeling of infinity'? John Stuart Mill once described the imaginative emotion as the feeling we get when 'an idea when vividly conceived excites in us'.[8] It is this excitement that we as teachers are challenged to create in our students. As Warnock comments 'Children cannot be taught to feel deeply; but they can be taught to look and listen in such a way that the imaginative emotion follows'.[9] How can we as educators teach this looking and listening, especially if we have not been well trained to cultivate it in our own disposition towards the world of the unknown?

This is not entirely a matter of individual choice: history and culture play an important role. Murphy (2010) argues that, historically, there are 'periodic golden ages of creativity' and key social institutions (universities, churches, councils, etc.) function as 'hand-maiden(s) to creation'.[10] So how does our own era fare on the creativity scale? Not very well.[11] Overall, 'the empirically measureable level of creativity in leading societies is less today than it was a century ago. The emphasis on bureaucratic management, and in a more general sense on procedure and procedural ideologies, is part of the reason for this'.[12] Although historically periods of creativity rise and wane, since 1870 the trend towards creativity has not been sustained. However, in that time, the public discourse and the gadgetry of creativity have exploded. Murphy offers this observation:

> We are less creative than we were 140 years ago. But we tell ourselves the obverse of this. The rhetoric of the creative society has become a consolation

for a decline of creative intensity. Ever-more sophisticated means of mechanical and digital distribution, remediation, and recycling of ideas have masked the fact that creative copyright and patent industries and institutions, not least of all the universities, produce fewer and fewer serious works per capita at greater and greater cost per unit.[13]

We who work as teachers can only perform our jobs within the confines imposed on us. And therein lies a struggle. Here I am reminded of the time many years ago when my son was about 6 years old. I asked him what had happened at school that day. He responded by telling me what that days' 'learning objectives' had been. My heart sank. I felt that I had allowed this creative spirit to be caged. I was not then, nor have I ever been convinced that stating and restating learning objectives brings us any closer to 'the feeling of infinity' which lies at the heart of imagination.

Children's author David Almond, himself a teacher of considerable experience, caused much heated debate in the United Kingdom when he suggested that '10% of the curriculum needs to be left as space, as dreamtime'.[14] He passionately criticises the government's educational policy, which leaves little room and no time for children to discover for themselves what lies within and beyond themselves, the stuff of their own dreams. Quoting William Blake, he asks 'How can a bird that is born for joy Sit in a cage and sing'?[15]

BECOMING AND BEING A TEACHER/LEARNER

Looking back now, it seems as if I always wanted to be a teacher. My teaching career began when I was about 6 years old and had just entered formal schooling. Wanting to share all that I had learned in the day with my younger siblings, I set up 'School Molly'. They would return home from nursery, and have to endure a lesson with me. But their efforts were handsomely rewarded; nearly all of their 'work' was handed back, with exuberant praise, and received marks in the range of A+++++++, and so they tolerated me. However, my first formal teaching experience was in the state school system in Cambridge, Massachusetts, where I taught history to students between the ages of 12 and 14. Till this day, I still have some of the cards which they made me when I left the school. Perhaps favorite amongst my momentos from that time, however, was a drawing I confiscated from one of my students, which I found him making during class. He was a talented artist, and his illustration was a detailed depiction of a battleship, with its name imprinted on the bow: SS Andrews. I kept this displayed on my desk for the rest of the year, and three decades later, I still have it.

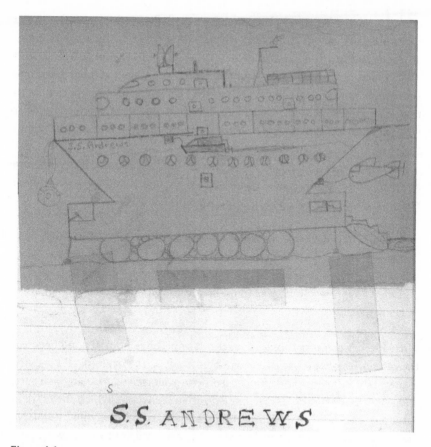

Figure 4.1:
I confiscated this elaborate drawing from a student when I was a school teacher, and had it on my desk for the rest of the year.

But in fact my pathway into becoming a teacher was not nearly so linear as the impression this synopsis might give. It was not only that I collected other jobs and research degrees along the way, but it was some years after I had been teaching that I realized that much of my sense of who I was, and am, was bound up with the profession of teaching. Like many pathways in life, I do not feel that the process of becoming a teacher is one which has a beginning and an ending. For me at least, I feel that my teaching is something which requires constant vigilance. Although certainly one gains great satisfaction if feedback on a particular course is positive—and stricken if the obverse is the case—nonetheless we are always recreating ourselves, and re-dedicating ourselves to making an environment in which learning can happen. All terms come to an end, and regardless of how well or poorly a course ran in any particular year, there will always be a another 'first day', where one must begin anew. That one cannot rest on one's laurels, so to speak, keeps us forever challenged; just as the moon rises and falls, so we know that we will always, yet again, have to begin at the beginning in our efforts to create the conditions for learning. And while much of the content we will teach may be largely similar from one year to the next, we are always somewhat changed by our experiences in the classroom. And so we should be. It is this reconstituted teaching self who will stand before the new class on that first day—and so the cycle of forever becoming a teacher continues.

But the category of teacher is one that is wholly relational. If there are no students, there are no teachers, and vice versa. They, and we, exist only in relation to one another. As Freire has argued

> There is no teaching without learning... teaching and learning take place in such a way that those who teach learn... because they recognize previously learned knowledge... and... because by observing how the novice student's curiosity works to apprehend what is taught... they help themselves to uncover uncertainties, rights, and wrongs.[16]

What Freire's comment underlines is not only the relational bond between the categories of teacher and learner, but indeed the overlap: all teachers, if they are to be effective, must also open themselves to being learners, and learners for their part are imbued with a knowledge which they can, in turn, share with others. Freire's model of education is a highly interactive one, in which the pursuit of knowledge is a shared venture between people. He critiques what he calls 'the banking concept of education' whereby teachers have knowledge which they impart to students, who are passive receptacles. Freire's view of education builds from models such as those articulated by Rousseau in the 18th century, with his theory of active learning, and more recently of John Dewey writing more than one hundred years later, who again promoted the idea that learning only happens when students are actively engaged in the construction of knowledge.

Freire summarized the relationship between educators and learners as 'complex, fundamental, and difficult; it is a relationship about which we should think constantly'.[17] For Freire, teaching is not a mere exercise of bonding between teacher and student. Indeed, he writes extensively criticizing over-indulgent teachers who ultimately cannot sufficiently exert themselves to be demanding of their students. '...one should never reduce teaching to merely a feel-good process, particularly to a paternalistic nurturing that takes the form of parental coddling'.[18] We owe our students more than bringing them comfort. As Hargreaves and Goodson write: 'Every learner needs a teacher who not only supports them, but also demands the best of them—morally, as well as intellectually'.[19] Good teaching is demanding for all who are involved.

There is, in fact, no simple formula for successful teaching. Research into former students' views on inspirational teachers does not reveal any predilection towards any particular style or content of teaching. Rather, what students appear to respond to is a teacher's ability to communicate the interrelatedness between their teaching, their research, and their lives. Parker Palmer calls this a 'capacity for connectedness'

> [Good teachers] are able to weave a complex web of connections among themselves, their subjects, and their students so that students can learn to weave a world for themselves. The methods used by these weavers vary widely: lectures, Socratic dialogues, laboratory experiments, collaborative problem solving, creative chaos. The connections made by good teachers are not in their methods but in their hearts....[20]

Two facets of this connectedness merit particular attention: (1) the personal connection between teachers and students—the possibilities and difficulties associated with a meeting of different worlds; and (2) the connection between teaching and research.

'KNOWING RELATIONSHIPS': ACCESSING THE WORLD OF OTHERS

As a young teacher starting out in his profession, Ivor Goodson kept a diary of his experience in the classroom. In his notes, he writes that

> ...the first stage in the learning process is the establishment of a 'knowing' relationship. The socio-pastoral threshold precedes the academic threshold... Without this relationship, whatever the pedagogy, transmission or transformation, there will be undue numbers of failures.... But the relationship is not just the prerequisite for transmission. It should by its establishment affect the nature of that transmission. The critical point is that at which the child engages, from then on exploration is cooperative. Learning becomes a possibility.[21]

In order for teachers and students to understand one another, they must, as Goodson suggests, have some sense of one another. The same words uttered by different people might well mean different things; our process of interpretation and internalization is intricately bound up with our perception of the social location of the speaker. Indeed, this is a basic premise upon which we lead our daily lives—varying not only what we say, but how we say it according to our sense of our audience. As listeners, we hear things differently according to how we read the speaker. How do these dynamics, with which we are all well practiced, translate into the classroom?

Sometimes teachers and students come from the same community, but often this is not the case. My experience of teaching at the University of East London is an example of the latter. In my department, 93% of the students are not white, many have either immigrated to the UK themselves, or are the children of parents who have done so. Many are Muslim, some of whom dress traditionally and some of whom do not. Almost all our students are working class. I, on the hand, am a nonreligious Jewish American woman from a well-educated, upper-middle-class family. I have attended some of the most elite universities in the world, and live in a town which is dominated by one of them, some 55 miles from where I teach. To put it simply, my students and I have very different experiences of the world. However, I do not feel that those differences impede the possibility of us creating together a rich learning environment. On the contrary, the range of lives which are assembled in one classroom as we try to intellectually unpick one concept or another makes for a far more stimulating engagement than if we all shared a common background.

Perhaps it is because of the kind of topics that I teach that this is not only implicit, but at certain moments, explicit. In the last chapter, I described the exercise I do in the beginning of my class on aging, in which students describe in detail the image that comes to their mind when they are asked to imagine an older person. The following week's exercise builds on this: they are asked to interview three people (one 'young', one 'middle-aged', and one 'old') about what aging means to them. The age boundaries of the three categories are not specified, and thus the age of those who appear in the different groups varies widely. (I cannot help but smile when someone who is 45 years old is interviewed as an old person!) But beyond the mere difference in age of those who are interviewed, the interviewees often come from different countries and have a wide range of experiences and expectations which influence their thoughts on aging. Each student is instructed to write up (briefly) the three interviews, and to bring their descriptions to class. The conversation, which develops from this rich mélange of materials is always very lively, as students are especially keen to hear about the conversations their classmates have had.

Another example of how the external world of my students enters into the classroom is in the course I teach on Life Histories. Here, not only do students spend an entire term doing a project on the life of one person—who they effectively 'bring into' the class, through the ongoing discussion of their coursework—but there are a series of smaller exercises which are designed to develop their skills along the way. The first of these happens in Week One. Students are given the instructions: 'In about 500 words, write a story about something that happened to you in your past. The event can be as small or large as you wish. Be aware that someone else will read your story'. The following week, they bring two copies of their stories to class, and we use these personal narratives as a vehicle for sensitizing students to questions of how people select certain stories and not others to tell about their lives, the dynamic temporality of representation, and other issues which are relevant to life-history research. The stories which I have collected over the years through this exercise range from the smallest of encounters, to detailed descriptions of personal traumatic events. (The stories are anonymous, though some students do make their identity known). The last time I taught this class, the students asked me to create a link on our course website where students could deposit their own narratives, and read those of others who had contributed. I was quite taken by their desire to know about the experiences of one another.

This request for a group link in which to deposit materials was repeated slightly later in the term when it came to the 20-minute interviewing exercise. Although I usually leave the topic for the interview completely open, that particular year I chose a focus. The class began only weeks after the London Riots, which I knew had affected the lives of many of our students. I gave them the following instructions: 'Interview someone for 20 minutes about an experience the individual had between the days of August 6–10, 2011, the days of the "London riots." Bring two copies of the transcript with you to class next week'. The stories which were brought in to the classroom through these interviews were extraordinary, not in their depiction of high drama (though some did veer in this direction) but more because of the power derived from their collectivity. The government approved the use of water cannons for the first time on British mainland, and overall, more than 3,000 people were arrested, some of whom received very harsh custodial sentences. David Cameron gave this analysis: 'There are pockets of our society that are not only broken, but frankly sick...It is a complete lack of responsibility in parts of our society, people allowed to feel that the world owes them something'. But the stories which were collected by the students in my classroom told a very different tale. The following excerpt from one interview demonstrates this:

> R: Straight away I had a sense of it being um...like really...I kind of...I didn't feel "what are those looters doing?", "why are they doing this? "Put them in jail", "Poor police guys"...I didn't. I kind of more sympathized with the people that were doing it. The rioters...not

the looters. But the people in the riots, the rioters, because they have a different like um…mindset behind it. Cos I think, I mean seriously they don't have…I mean, I can definitely understand why this is going on—it's a political thing, it's frustration of…They have never ever been…no one has ever ever looked to their side of things or given them…they're not really a part of the society in some ways. No one really thinks like they do. Cos no one in power would ever be able to know how their situation is. So I was a bit, that's what I instantly felt like. I can actually understand this.

T: So you seem to have a lot of sympathy with the rioters, would you say that?

R: Yeah, yeah I do.

T: Do you think what they were doing can be justified?

R: I actually think it can be justified. It is…I don't know if I can say that it wasn't right. The looting wasn't right, the rioting was right and that can be justified.

The viewpoint expressed in this excerpt reveals a framework of meaning which resonates with many of my students, insisting on a distinction between protest ('rioting') and breaking the law ('looting'). Many of them share the feeling that 'no one has ever ever looked to their side of things'. The condemnation by the government was swift and severe, but as this speaker asks, would those who sit in harsh judgement 'ever be able to know how their situation is'? Although the exercise was ostensibly designed to develop students' skills as interviewers, at the same time (and perhaps even primarily) it gave them the opportunity to discuss their experiences and interpretations of those tumultuous days.

I have provided these examples of classroom exercises to demonstrate ways in which students' worlds are explicitly called upon in some of the teaching which I do. I have always felt that if students are to develop a taste for a course of study, they must think it has relevance in the real world, indeed, in their real world. The path of intellectual exploration does not always end in personal experience, but it does often begin with it.

Indeed, if we are to show our students that what we wish to teach them has some relevance to their lives, then we must have a sense of what their lives consist of. As Freire writes:

…our relationship with the learners demands that we respect them and demands equally that we be aware of the concrete conditions of their world, the conditions that shape them. To try to know the reality that our students live is a task that the educational practice imposes on us: Without this, we have no access to the way they think, so only with great difficulty can we perceive what and how they know.[22]

Of course, it is not only through assignments and exercises that students reveal their worlds. This happens in a number of ways, including, as already mentioned, their classroom contributions. Invariably, they bring what and who they know into the class, and use this experience bank as the material they will work up into knowledge.

Silence and non-participation can be the result of a wide range of reasons including lack of sleep, lack of interest, lack of preparation, and distraction (from within and beyond the classroom). In my experience, it is always best to explore with the student what is happening in their lives before assuming anything. Several years ago I came across one of my students in the library, barely able to keep her eyes open, yet determined to continue with her work (for my class, as it turned out). I sat and spoke with her. She told me that in order to support her education, her children, and her family back in her country of origin, she held a night job. Each day after finishing her classes at university, she would go home to feed her children, and then go out to work, which did not finish till 6 a.m. She would then sleep for two hours, before returning to university in time for her 9 a.m. class. This schedule had begun to catch up with her. Together we made a plan which enabled her both to complete her work and to get the rest she so obviously needed. She not only completed the class, but was the recipient of the outstanding student award of our university, for students who meet their commitments in extraordinary circumstances.

On another occasion, there was a young woman who had begun my class with great enthusiasm. She was vibrant, and beautiful, and obviously someone who gave much attention to how she dressed. (She had a wide range of brilliantly coloured hijabs, which she coordinated meticulously with her make-up and nail varnish). Suddenly she became very quiet and withdrawn. I asked her to come see me. When she did so, at first she offered no explanation. We sat for a while and spoke more generally. After some time, it emerged that she had been raped by a family friend. She could not tell her parents for fear that they would punish, if not disown her. She feared she might be pregnant. Meanwhile, the family friend was someone she had to continue to see in the home where she was living. How could she be expected to focus on her studies when her life was falling apart? In the months that followed we spent a lot of time together. I helped her to make contact with the medical and support services she required. In the end, she not only was able to complete my class, but her degree. When I last saw her, at her graduation, she seemed to be on the road to rebuilding her life.

Over the years, I have encountered many such stories from my students. But equally, I never cease to be moved by their depths of determination, courage and resilience. Some of them have made quite extraordinary steps to end up where they are—in my classroom—overcoming obstacles (personal and financial) just to be there, at university. I am acutely aware of the distance between my world and theirs, and know that I have much to learn from them. Equally I know I must always be worthy of being their teacher, rendering the sacrifices they have made to be there worthwhile. As Greene (2003) writes: 'Teaching is possibility in dark and constraining times'.[23]

NARRATING THE LIVES OF TEACHERS: THE SEARCH FOR BALANCE

And what of my life do I share with them? bell hooks describes the importance of teachers being willing not only to listen and learn from the worlds of their students, but being willing to expose themselves.

> When education is the practice of freedom, students are not the only ones who are asked to share, to confess. Engaged pedagogy does not seek simply to empower students. Any classroom that employs a holistic model of learning will also be a place where teachers grow, and are empowered by the process. That empowerment cannot happen if we refuse to be vulnerable while encouraging students to take risks.... When professors bring narratives of their experiences into classroom discussions it eliminates the possibility that we can function as all-knowing, silent interrogators.[24]

Getting the balance right is difficult, and one must constantly reassess what is most appropriate for any particular situation. Although my general inclination is to bring myself in to the classroom, I am also aware that there are limitations to this. Ultimately students have enrolled to study a particular discipline, not to emerge as experts on our lives. Yet using personal experience (theirs as well as my own) can be very effective as tools for accessing abstract concepts. For example, when teaching developmental psychology, I am quite prepared to draw on examples from my own life as a mother of two teenagers.[25] In my class on aging, where students are expected to talk about the meaning that age has for them and those they know, I think it is important that I am willing to do the same. (I was particularly touched one year when my birthday fell on the day of class, and they brought in a cake and even sang to me.)

Ivor Goodson has used the term 'pedagogic moments' to describe those times when

> ... the rupture between teaching as a life and living a life was not inevitable. In
> the pedagogic moment, the rupture between teachers and taught is healed and
> a dialectic, an exchange, takes place, which affects not just beliefs but the very
> heart of the matter of living and experience.[26]

Reading Goodson's compelling description, there was one example which came immediately to my mind. Several years ago, an extraordinary postgraduate student of ours died in a tragic accident over the Easter holidays. As fate would have it, the very first lecture I had to give upon my return was in my class on the sociology of aging, on the topic of death and dying. I had prepared my teaching materials before the vacation, but as I reviewed them the day before the class, the enormity of the task became increasingly palpable to me. Although as undergraduates my students did not know the student who had died, I was aware that several of them had had their own recent and painful losses. How could we together integrate these experiences into our classroom? I began the class on a personal note. I told them what had happened over the holidays with our postgraduate student, and I acknowledged the recent losses which some of them had experienced. Slowly and carefully we began to talk, using the reading for the week (Jean Amery's extraordinary piece 'To Live with Dying') as a vehicle for coming to terms with the all-too-real experiences of our lives. The atmosphere of the classroom was utterly charged, as together we helped each other to think about this most difficult of topics.

The physical space of my small office also reveals parts of my life. As Welby Ings writes:

> ... the wall of my office is graced with small objects... eclectic scavengings, the
> detritus of many journeys... small gifts I have been given because students
> know my penchant for the unusual and neglected. They help me to think.[27]

Although I cannot claim, as Ings implies, that I have objects with intrinsic anthropological value, my office is an intimate place, covered with photos, posters, and endless objects, which together weave a story of who I am. There are signs from demonstrations against the education cuts, gifts from students (amongst my favorites: a carpet from Iran, a silver tree of life from Turkey, a small, vibrant textile created by one of them), Happy Birthday decorations marking the tenth anniversary of our research centre, and of

Figure 4.2:
My office.

course the kettle and assorted mugs (some with their own stories). There is also an autobiographical collage hanging, which was made by our student who tragically died. And just at eye level from the chair where I sit, a postcard I have had with me since the days studying for my PhD, the picture of the earth as taken from outer space. This for me symbolizes the importance of keeping a sense of perspective—not only in terms of remembering that there might be good reasons why our students do not meet the deadlines we set for them, but also, and at the same time, being mindful of the sense of infinity which it is our duty as teachers to communicate.

In the past three decades, there has been an increasing interest not only in teacher training, but more specifically in teachers' lives. Goodson (1981) summarizes the importance of this topic 'in understanding something so intensely personal as teaching, it is critical we know about the person the teacher is'.[28] In this vein, there has been some very creative and robust research with, on and by teachers, examining the interconnections and ruptures between the lives they lead and who they are as educators. Clandinin et al.[29] have explored the importance of personal stories to teachers, students, administrators and families as they all try to make sense of one another. All these stories are interwoven into the identity of the school. The authors identify a 'network of stories' which combine to make a 'landscape of stories'. The stories are themselves forever changing, and are '... rooted temporally as individual stories shift and change

Figure 4.3:
This photo helps to put life's daily trials in to perspective.

in response to changing events and circumstances. Changes in the story of school and school stories ripple through the school and influence the whole web of stories'.[30] Clearly, one important thread in the web of stories is that of the teachers. Exploring the meaning of identity of their professional identity, teachers ask themselves

> ... questions such as 'Who am I in my story of teaching?', 'Who am I in my place in the school?', 'Who am I in the children's stories?' This attention to identity led them to develop a narrative concept of 'stories to live by' to conceptually bring together personal practical knowledge, professional knowledge landscapes, and teacher identity.[31]

So far, I have argued for the importance for teachers both to learn about the life worlds of their students, and to be willing to bring aspects of their own lives in to the classroom. But all does not reduce to personal stories, neither those of our students nor our own. As Goodson warns (2005):

> Personal and practical teachers' stories may... act not to further our understandings, but merely to celebrate the particular constructions of the 'teacher' which have been wrought by political and social contestation. Teachers' stories can be stories of particular political victories and political settlement. Because of the limitation of focus, teachers' stories—as stories of the personal and practical— are likely to be limited in this manner.[32]

Although there is much to be learned by close investigation into the lives of teachers and the stories they tell, at the same time there is a risk of this focus 'reduc[ing] the oxygen of broader understandings. The breathing space comes to look awfully like a vacuum, where history and social construction are somehow suspended'.[33]

It is important to remember why we have been brought together: we have a responsibility to our students to teach them (even while we acknowledge that in doing so, we ourselves learn). Establishing a knowing relationship with our students might, as Goodson suggests, be a pre-requisite to learning, but it is only that. How can we instil in others a passion for our subject?

IGNITING CURIOSITY FOR THE SUBJECT

Marcus du Sautoy, the Simonyl Professor for the Public Understanding of Science and Professor of Mathematics at Oxford University, describes himself as a young child as someone who showed no particular talent for the subject; till this day he describes himself as 'hopeless about multiplication tables and things like that'. It was an inspiring teacher, "Mr. Bells", who showed him that Maths could be more than numeracy and long division.

> I was about 12 or 13, and this teacher at my comprehensive school took me aside at the end of my lesson and said 'Look, I think you should find out what Maths is really about' and he started to show me things about prime numbers, symmetry, topology, and it just sort of opened up my eyes to what a beautiful world this was. He kind of gave me this key to a secret garden and I've been running around in it ever since.[34]

Unlocking a world is a great gift, and it is my feeling that we succeed as teachers if students leave our classrooms wanting to find out more about the subject. Clearly, not all students will feel equally drawn to the subjects we teach—that is simply human nature. The most that we as teachers can hope for is that we will make our students sufficiently curious about whatever it is we are teaching that they will seek to find out more. Although there are many different factors which might contribute to such an outcome, I believe that first amongst them is that the teacher must herself be passionate about her subject. When this is not the case, it is incumbent upon us to find a way to make the topic interesting, first to ourselves. Without this, the class stands little chance of being anything other than a marking of time. As I have written earlier: 'A teacher who has grown numb to her subject matter is not one who will ignite a flame of intellectual passion in others. Interest and enthusiasm are not always contagious, but they are often so'.[35]

Of course, in order to nourish imagination in one's students, one must have the preparedness to see it. Moat (2012a) argues that many teachers are themselves so beaten down by the system, their own imaginations are being starved of air. When this is so,

> ... it is unreal to suppose they could find time or energy to foster their own self-expressive imaginative lives. The consequence is predictable enough—teachers come to view the Imagination not as a reality in their own lives, but as some technical application that can be ear-marked and graded by the system. As a result they are often taken out of their depth by the raw, unruly Imagination of their students, are perhaps intimated, and haven't the experience to either encourage or discipline it.[36]

We owe it not only to ourselves, but to our students, to protect the roots of our own creativity.

Fried (2003) suggests that passionate teaching is not just something we offer our students. It is also a gift we grant ourselves: a way of honoring our life's work, our profession. It says: 'I know why I am devoting this life I've got to these [students]'.[37] He then proceeds to make two observations about passionate teachers:

> 1. [they] organize and focus their passionate interests by getting to the heart of their subject and sharing with their students some of what lies there—the beauty and power that drew them to this field in the first place and that has deepened over time as they have learned and experienced more...
>
> 2. [they] convey their passion to novice learners—their students—by acting as partners in learning, rather than as 'experts in the field'. As partners, they invite less experienced learners to search for knowledge and insightful experiences, and they build confidence and competence among students who might otherwise choose to sit back and watch their teacher do and say interesting things.[38]

If we are to be effective teachers we need to ensure that our own love of our subject is kept alive, and like all loves, that requires an ongoing commitment to work for it. Even the most fascinating of topics can run dry if one only performs as one who is intellectually engaged, rather than ensuring that indeed that is the case, and not just a vestige from a time passed. Fried's second observation—that passionate teachers enter into intellectual 'partnerships' with their students rather than presenting themselves as individuals whose own knowledge journey is complete—is equally important, particularly in light of the responsibility of teachers to train tomorrow's scholars. But how do we do this?

With all the technological advances which have made different kinds of teaching possible—and they are considerable—we are challenged to be forever vigilant about our purpose of educating. How can we best avail ourselves of the tools which enhance our ability to touch the imagination of our students—through recordings, videos, music, and more—while not suffocating them with unprocessed information? The German philosopher and theologian Friedrich Schleiermacher, writing at the end of the 19th century, made the important distinction between the transmission and the production of knowledge. He argued that students should not 'collect knowledge but rather directly observe the activity of "reason" as it creates knowledge'.[39] Believing such, Schleiermacher was scathing on the state of the practice of lecturing.

> Few understand the significance of using lectures, but, oddly enough, this practice has always persevered despite its constantly being very poorly done by the majority of teachers... it is worth the trouble to reserve this form of instruction always for those few who, from time to time, know how to handle it correctly. Indeed one could say that the true and peculiar benefit a university teacher confers is always in exact relation to the person's proficiency in this art.[40]

Inviting our students into a world in which they can observe 'the activity of reason' demands that we demonstrate ourselves before them as scholars. As Murphy comments: 'The professor's primary function is not to transmit knowledge but to provide an observable and imitable model of how to produce knowledge'.[41]

If this is the case, and I believe it to be so, why is it that so often teaching and research are referred to as antithetical activities? It is most unfortunate that we have lost the view that these domains of our professional life share much common ground between them. Loeffler (2011) describes his teaching: 'I teach my students like the mountains teach me. With vision. With struggle. Asking them to reach up and out and to reach for an unknown sky. To learn while filled with uncertainty and sometimes with joy and mirth'.[42] The characteristics which he lists here (vision, struggle, reaching for the unknown, the uncertainty and joy of learning) are all equally integral to the pursuit of scholarly research. An important aspect of teaching is mentoring—showing our students, through our own example, how to connect the world of ideas with practical knowledge and with real, lived experience. Perhaps this is why John Moat feels that 'an eagerness to teach, or act mentor, is most often an attribute of realised imaginative authority'.[43]

Not only is my teaching enhanced by my research, but my research is more grounded when I sensitize myself to the complex process by which we, and I, come to know things. In the very act of teaching, we must take ourselves through the steps of relearning our subject, and in so doing making the familiar strange to us once again. This allows us to reacquaint ourselves with our own intellectual journeys, shedding a new perspective on that which we might have come to take for granted. Many scholars rely on teaching as a source of training those with whom they will conduct their research. Moreover, in the broadest sense, teaching secures scholarship for the future. Without curious minds working with us and challenging us, without those who will carry on after we have gone, our scholarship is destined to evaporate in a dead end. Teaching is the thread that connects our scholarship to tomorrow, even while research is the fire which keeps our teaching fresh, even sometimes inspiring.

TEACHING FOR DEMOCRATIC CITIZENSHIP

Throughout this chapter, I have spoken of the importance of keeping oneself forever mindful of why we are teaching. Integral to this question is what it is that we feel we are preparing our students for. There is an instrumental response to this question: students attend university not only to learn more about the world around them, but often primarily as a means to an end—in the belief that a university degree will help them to procure better employment. But even while that response is legitimate, it is insufficient. We are engaged in education because we believe that it matters, not only to the individuals who enter our classrooms, but to all of us. Through education we learn what democratic citizenship means; as Wolfgang Edelstein argues, this 'is not just an extension of the serious business of learning for life. It is the serious business of learning for life and, as such, it must be a central goal of education'.[44]

In her book *Not for Profit*, American philosopher Martha Nussbaum identifies what she sees as 'a worldwide crisis in education.' She expands on this:

> The future of the world's democracies hangs in the balance...the humanistic aspects of science and social science—the imaginative, creative aspect, and the aspect of rigorous critical thought—are...losing ground as nations prefer to pursue short-term profit by the cultivation of the useful and highly applied skills suited to profit-making.[45]

If our first challenge is to connect with our students and to enable them to think critically about the world they know, then our greatest challenge is to extend their thought to what lies beyond the familiar. At the heart of this is learning how to live in a world of different others, recognizing that one's location, with its particular claims, is just one amongst millions.

Nussbaum (2010) lists a number of abilities which she feels citizens must have if the nation is to promote a type of 'humane, people-sensitive democracy'.[46] Amongst these abilities, she includes three which are particularly germane to the discussion here:

- The ability to imagine well a variety of complex issues affecting the story of a human life as it unfolds: to think about childhood, adolescence, family relationships, illness, death, and much more in a way informed by an understanding of a wide range of human stories, not just by aggregate data.
- The ability to think about the good of the nation as a whole, not just that of one's own local group.
- The ability to see one's own nation, in turn, as a part of a complicated world order in which issues of many kinds require intelligent transnational deliberation for their resolution.[47]

Clearly what Nussbaum identifies here is a graduated ability to take the perspective of others—something which has long been associated with psychological and moral development.[48,49] In order to perform the essential task of 'cultivating humanity', individuals require the capacity to be able to reflect critically upon their own lives and traditions, and to adopt an international perspective in which all human lives are connected. Although these two capacities are important, they are not enough to be able to transport an individual into the frame of meaning of another person, whose life circumstances may be very different from one's own. For this, citizens require what Nussbaum has called 'the narrative imagination'.

> This means the ability to think what it might be like to be in the shoes of a person different from oneself, to be an intelligent reader of that person's story, and to understand the emotions and wishes and desires that someone so placed might have.[50]

It is the exercise of this imagination that gives individuals the tools to decipher meaning from another person's perspective. It is not surprising that Nussbaum points to the power of storytelling to awaken this imagination. 'As we tell stories about the lives of others, we learn how to imagine what another creature might feel in response to various events. At the same time, we identify with the other creature and learn something about ourselves'.[51]

Through learning about others, we learn about ourselves as our world is revealed to us as just one possible way of living. Critically, Nussbaum argues that accessing the real-life worlds of others requires more than logic and reasoning; without trying to put ourselves in the shoes of others, we remove the possibility of developing a sympathetic understanding of them.

The claim that world citizens need to develop a 'sympathetic imagination' is not new. As Nussbaum points out, nearly two thousand years ago, Marcus Aurelius insisted that it was our capacity for sympathetic imagination that '...enable[s] us to comprehend the motives and choices of people different from ourselves, seeing them not as forbiddingly alien and other, but as sharing many problems and possibilities with us'.[52]

Still, as argued in the early pages of this book, all imaginations are situated, and one can only ever imagine the position of another from one's own point of view. How can we make sure that we do not collapse all existing differences between ourselves and others, so that ultimately all that remains is what we hold in common (or which we imagine we hold in common?) Modell (2003) in his study on the relationship between imagination and the brain, comments upon the importance of empathy:

> Empathy involves a sense of similarity while maintaining a sense of difference... our cognitive capacity to empathically know other minds relies on an unimpaired faculty for metaphoric thought... the sense of the 'as if'... Identifying with the other rests on a paradox—that one is similar to the other and yet one remains oneself. One must be able to accept the paradox of something that both is and is not.[53]

It is our job within the classroom to nourish this all-important sense of metaphor, the world of 'as if'. We do this not only by the force of reason (though that plays a critical role). As Tagore once commented: 'We may become powerful by knowledge, but we attain fullness by sympathy'.[54]

How can we as teachers encourage our students to develop compassionate understanding (which Nussbaum argues is essential for civic responsibility), enhancing their ability to feel with another, even while recognizing their differences? First, we must have a sense of our own vulnerability, and from this position we are more open to the worlds of others.[55] Even while 'we cannot actually know what it is like to be somebody else' we can try, in the words of Hannah Arendt, 'to think with an enlarged mentality [which] means to train one's imagination to go visiting'.[56] The first step in this 'visiting' is to try to make strange that which is familiar to us. Following Sartre, 'the ability to imagine is identical with the ability to detach ourselves from our actual situation'.[57] This attempt to distance ourselves from ourselves, however difficult it might be, gives us a new platform from which to view not only our own situation but the world of others, both near and far.

Von Wright observes the difficulty involved in 'seeing difference' that is close to home:

> Confronting difference is easier when it happens in a remote place:... It seems to be easier to understand and include somebody who is different elsewhere, than to recognize differences in your own context and accept the otherness of one's neighbour. Why is that so?[58]

This challenging question brings us back in to the classroom, where the building of knowledge requires first that students and teachers create together an environment in which learning is a possibility. We as teachers have a delicate balance to strike: On the one hand, there is a body of knowledge which we want our students to access, to interact with, and to make their own. On the other hand, and in tension with the aim of certain knowledge, we want to nourish in our students an openness to the world, in Nussbaum's words,

> an ability to trust uncertain things beyond your own control... [the ethical life is] based on a trust in the uncertain and on a willingness to be exposed; it's based on being more like a plant than like a jewel, something rather fragile, but whose very particular beauty is inseparable from that.[59]

Reconciling 'synthetic imagination' with 'analytic reason' remains one of the most important challenges for educators.

Nussbaum comments that 'the moral imagination can often become lazy'[60]; 'the muscles of the imagination', she warns, require training. We must resist the temptation to assume that other lives (of people who live across the globe, or those who stand before us in our classroom) are just other versions of our own. 'Cultivating our humanity in a complex interlocking world involves understanding the ways in which common needs and aims are differently realized in different circumstances'.[61] In those rare moments when we as teachers successfully meet this difficult task, the rewards are great. As bell hooks writes:

> The classroom, with all of its limitations, remains a location of possibility. In that field of possibility we have the opportunity to labor for freedom, to demand of ourselves and our comrades, an openness of mind and heart that allows us to face reality even as we collectively imagine ways to move beyond boundaries, to transgress. This is education as the practice of freedom.[62]

It is because of this possibility that I answered as I did when my son asked me what job I would choose if I could have any. Like Ings (2011), my years of teaching have given me 'glimpses of the extraordinary limits to which people can take themselves if they learn that someone cares about them and believes in their ability to take control of their own thinking'[63]; for having the privilege to be part of this, I am very thankful.

CHAPTER 5

Politics

When Barack Obama re-entered the Capitol, having just been sworn in as the 44th President of the United States, and having delivered his second inaugural address, he suddenly stopped his entourage to turn back toward the cheering crowds gathered on the National Mall.

'"I want to take a look, one more time," he said. 'I'm not going to see this again'.[1]

That was exactly the way I felt—he wanted to see me, indeed us, again, but we wanted to see him too. My children and I had experienced 'history in the making' in 2009, flying across the Atlantic Ocean to witness Obama's inauguration. Although Obama's victory in 2012 felt different (you can only have 'the first time' once), it confirmed for many that 2008 had not been a fluke. As Obama explained:

> It was easy to think that maybe 2008 was the anomaly. And I think 2012 was an indication that, no, this is not an anomaly. We've gone through a very difficult time. The American people have rightly been frustrated at the pace of change, and the economy is still struggling, and this President we elected is imperfect. And yet despite all that, this is who we want to be. That's a good thing.[2]

We wanted to be there this time too. The day of inauguration was not as cold as it had been in 2009—a full 12 degrees warmer—and the crowds were not as thick (though still considerable, at an estimated 800,000 to 1 million, compared to, for instance, George W. Bush who attracted 300,000 and 400,000 for his first and second inaugurations, respectively). The souvenirs were different; not so many 'Hope' posters, and instead some rather novel 'Obama condoms', being advertised as 'the ultimate stimulus package', and t-shirts reading 'Ob—Obamium' as if it were a newly discovered element of the periodic table.

The centrepiece admidst all the crowds and pageantry was the inaugural speech—'Evolved, Unapologetic and Urgent' read the headlines of the *New York Times* the following day, which was 'suffused with the spirit of...of Rev. Dr. Martin Luther King Jr.'s calls to heed "the fierce urgency of now'.[3] One of the most memorable passages in this memorable speech was his declaration:

> We the people declare today that the most evident of truths—that all of us are created equal—is the star that guides us still, just as it guided our forebears through Seneca Falls and Selma and Stonewall; just as it guided all those men and women, sung and unsung, who left footprints along this great Mall, to hear a preacher say that we cannot walk alone, to hear a king proclaim that our individual freedom is inextricably bound to the freedom of every soul on Earth.[4]

Obama, evoking history as a clarion for addressing the pressing issues of our time; seamlessly connecting individual freedom to the freedom of all; telling stories as a means for galvanizing action. Nearing the end of his speech, Obama drove his message home: 'You and I, as citizens, have the power to set this country's course. You and I, as citizens, have the obligation to shape the debates of our time, not only with the votes we cast, but the voices we lift in defense of our most ancient values and enduring ideas'.[5] We are in this together, you and I, the President told his people. And what we do now connects us to our past and to our future. He was speaking to me, and to all Americans. The story he was weaving had enough room in it for all of us. '...[W]ith common effort and common purpose...let us answer the call of history'. And so his second term as president began.

If you walk into a bookstore, there are entire shelves dedicated to Barack Obama. The industry which has grown up around the Obama phenomena is very unusual for a living politician, and exceptional for someone who has only been on the international scene for less than a decade. Obama both embodies and embraces narrative,[6] and his appreciation and strategic use of stories in his leadership has been a critical aspect of the way in which he does politics. Writing just after Obama's 2009 inauguration, British journalist Robert McCrum comments: 'Rarely has there been such a moving exhibition of the narrative gene that lurks in our DNA...Obama...seems to understand that, as much as gorgeous language or big ideas, what matters is story, story, story, a national narrative'.[7]

It has been remarked by many that Obama is a great orator. Even those who do not support him acknowledge his gift of words, and sometimes try to use this as a launching pad for criticism against him. Paul Ryan, accepting the nomination on the Republican ticket to run as Mitt Romney's vice president in July 2012, commented to his audience: 'Ladies and gentlemen, these past four years we have suffered no shortage of words in the White House'.[8] The president was portrayed as being a man only of words, who lacked the ability to lead. This comment echoed those of other Republicans which had been made throughout Obama's first term. For instance, following the dramatic losses suffered by the Democrats in the 2010 midterm elections, Sarah Palin used the Obama language as a source of humour, a way to denigrate the high-sounding principles which had not yielded fruit as quickly as many had wished. 'This was all part of that hope and change and transparency. Now...I gotta ask the supporters of all that, "How's that hopey, changey stuff working out?" '[9] she asked.

Still, there are many who are drawn to Obama's gift for language. Writing in January 2009, historian Simon Schama declared 'Right now he owns American rhetoric'. Describing a speech Obama gave in January 2008, he wrote:

> Obama can play heart and he can play head. He's the classical orator as well as the preacher of call-and-response. That evening he was pitch-perfect; letting the emotional electricity surge before cooling the voltage. He spoke in calculated measures, light on his feet, the basketballing candidate with the nifty jump shot, head turned slightly aside as if tuning in to history's promptings: "I hear you Abe, I hear you Martin; message coming in loud and clear".[10]

Time and again, Obama has exhibited an exceptional appreciation of the importance of story to people's ideas of who they are, as individuals and as part of a larger whole. He has done this through a compelling telling and re-telling of his own personal voyage, his 'unlikely candidacy' as he terms this, which he has then tied up with a national narrative, a narrative which we Americans construct about ourselves ('we are a land where all things are possible' etc.) which is combined with a counterstory of an America which has lost its way. Into this multiple storytelling, Obama has brought not only his own story, but also the stories of millions of other Americans. He drew on stories explicitly in his campaign for the 2008 election, as volunteers throughout the country gathered in town halls, living rooms, and school auditoriums, inviting people to come and tell their stories, and to share those stories with others. Through this mechanism, Obama was able to build a sense of community which not only helped him to identify the issues which were closest to people's hearts—something he could have done just as easily by other forms of public polling—but which closely knit strangers to one another. People were made to feel that they, and their individual stories, were part of a larger whole, and that together, their stories counted. As a newly elected president, he did this in his concerted effort to gain support for his economic crisis plan, gathering tens of thousands of 'economic crisis' stories, which were made accessible to the public with only a click of the mouse. Online, one could select any state and read stories of how this crisis had impacted the lives of individuals, their families, and their communities. There were pictures of these people. The stories felt real. And the effect was powerful. Four years later, barackobama.com is sending out messages asking people to tell their story about what $2000 means to them—in an attempt to show support for Obama's tax plan not to raise taxes for the middle class. After outlining the issues, the message ends 'Your story matters and Congress needs to hear it... Thanks for speaking out'. The strategic use of political storytelling is a hallmark of the Obama presidency, and has been applied in virtually every key moment when he has needed to get his message across to the American people.

POLITICAL NARRATIVES: SOME BACKGROUND

The opening decade of the 21st century has been marked by an increasing interest in what can broadly be termed 'political narratives',[11-17] a phenomenon which can perhaps be seen as one manifestation of the ballooning study of narrative more generally within the social sciences. Stories are one of the most effective tools which individuals and communities have for making sense of themselves and the world around them, and as such the study of the relationship between narrative and politics is vital. As Selbin (2011) writes:

> People rely on stories to make sense of their world, their place in it, and their (im)possibilities.... stories reflect and refract people's lives in a way that almost no other text can, making the abstract concrete, the complex more manageable, and rendering matters 'real'. Stories reduce the immense complexity of the world, involving our daily lives, to human-sized matters, adding information to stores that are already stocked, fitting by and large into familiar pathways.[18]

Although there is no strict consensus over what is and is not to be regarded as political narrative, there appears to be a general agreement that stories—both personal and communal—are pivotal to the way in which politics operates, both in people's minds (i.e. how they understand politics, and their place within and outside of the formal political sphere) as well as to how politics is practiced.[19] For a policy to be effective, there needs to be a reasonable story for why it is needed, or why another response would be inadequate or inappropriate. These stories, as it were, are not just within the domain of the individual, but are built upon the collective memory of a group, just as they help to create how that memory is mobilised and for what purposes. And critically, narratives are central to the machination of politics, for in constructing the stories about what is and isn't working, and how this compares to a notion of 'how it should be', we are invariably deciding what aspects of social/political/economic/ cultural life are and are not relevant to the current problem and its solu- tion—in other words, the lifeblood of politics. Thus, political narratives engage the imagination, not only in constructing stories about the past and the present, but in helping to articulate a vision of an alternative world. As Marqusee (2012) writes:

> We need utopian thinking if we are to engage successfully in the critical battle
> over what is or is not possible, if we are to challenge what are presented as immu-
> table 'economic realities'. Without a clear alternative—the outlines of a just and
> sustainable society—we are forced to accept our opponent's parameters.[20]

All these stories—constructions of the past, present, and future—only ever exist in relation to other stories, and politics is nothing if not a stage for competing stories to be told about the same phenomena.

So what are political narratives? What do they actually look like, and how can we recognise them when we see them? Elsewhere, I have described political narratives as the 'stories people tell about how the world works, how they explain the engines of political change, and the role they see themselves, and those whom they regard as being part of their group, as playing in this ongoing struggle'.[21] But the meaning of the term 'polit- ical narrative' is not limited to stories which are told or untold, lived, dreamed or imagined by individuals. Rather, it can also refer to a larger cluster of national stories, within which individuals position themselves, explicitly or otherwise. Discussion of political narratives always turns to an examination of the relationship between macro and micro narratives, in other words the relationship between the stories of individuals and the stories of the communities in which they live. Political narratives which individuals tell may or may not be explicitly about politics; often the most telling of them are not. But in the stories which they weave, individuals reveal how they position themselves within the communities in which they live, to whom or what they see themselves as belonging to/alienated from, how they construct notions of power, and the processes by which such power is negotiated. For individuals, political narratives are the ligaments of identity, revealing how one constructs the boundaries of, and the connections between, the self and the other. Hannah Arendt has argued that storytelling is 'the bridge by which we transform that which is private and individual into that which is public, and in this capactity, it is one of the key components of social life'.[22] 'What makes mass society so difficult to bear is... the fact that the world has lost its power to gather [people] together, to relate and to separate them'.[23] Political narratives are vital in establishing these relational bonds.

However, one could also make an observation of the reverse trend; that is, one of the stumbling blocks to realising social change in modern times has been a tendency to over-personalise issues which should remain in the sphere of the public/political domain. Zingaro (2009) describes an 'emotional economy' in which there is an 'offering up of "the real story" of trauma, pain, or humiliation, from someone who has "been there".[24] Although such stories might be able to provide particular insight into difficult experiences, their telling depends upon the existence of a willing, listening audience. Knowledge which is 'too threatening or too different from the listener's experience' is suspect: 'A story without recognizable landmarks, or some measure of a familiar narrative trajectory, marks the teller as lying, or possibly exaggerating'.[25] Stories always exist in relation to other stories, of individuals and communities, and they rely upon these bonds in order to be 'tellable'. Political stories, even when they relate to individual experience, are never just the property of isolated selves.

In the life of the community, political narratives play a number of key functions. In times of traumatic rupture, the construction of a story about the past can be regarded as the first and most critical step in moving out of the darkness. This is the basic premise upon which some truth commissions have been established. The Truth and Reconciliation Commission (TRC) of South Africa attempted to piece together a 'tellable past' through the collection of more than 22,000 personal narratives in which individuals recounted what abuses they and their loved ones had suffered during key moments in the apartheid era (specifically between the Soweto massacre of 1961 and the first democratic election in 1994). Desmond Tutu, who chaired the TRC, commented at the first victim hearing:

> We pray that all those people who have been injured in either body or spirit may receive healing through the work of this commission... We are charged to unearth the truth about our dark past. To lay the ghosts of that past, so that they will not return to haunt us and that we will hereby contribute to the healing of a traumatized and wounded people.[26]

Central to the construction of the TRC was that storytelling, even about horrific events, could perform a healing function, if not for individuals, then at least for communities who must now find a way to live together.

Though the actual act of narrating a painful past may cause additional suffering, it is also true that finding commonality with the stories of others can itself bring a measure of satisfaction, even agency. As Hannah Arendt writes: 'The presence of others who see what we see and hear what we hear assures us of the reality of the world and ourselves'.[27] Political narratives play a critical role in creating and recreating history—at the level of the individual, the community, and the nation. In as much as identity is inextricably linked to story, and is forever a project in the making, political narratives are, by extension, a mechanism through which the past is reformulated in light of a desired future.

Finally, political narratives are strategically employed in the construction of national identity. Through the use of political narratives, we tell our selves and others who we are (and as observed above, these stories change over time). These are the hardships we have endured; these are the principles for which we stand; these are rewards which we as a people have procured. Our group-identity claims rest upon our stories. And these stories are then represented in a myriad of ways, including statues, public celebrations, memorialisation, and in history lessons.

National narratives are not synonymous with political narratives, though there is a significant overlap between them. However, not all political narratives concern matters of the nation, and many national narratives are about culture, or art, for instance. Although politics encompasses the broad spectrum of stories about power—who has it; how it is shared or abused; the particular contexts which inform its various manifestations, etc.—national narratives are concerned with those negotiations which happen explicitly around questions of the nation. Questions of national identity are invariably linked to national narratives. Nations are communities, both real and imagined, and from the time they are very young, people develop a sense of what it means to be from this place, a sense of belonging and/or alienation, an evaluation of how things run, who has control over what, and how that control is exercised. National narratives are both general (this is who we are as a people) and specific (this is what it means to me to be from here), and are manifest in both formal and informal ways. National identity can be expressed either in a formal, public context (such as the statues, national holidays, and history books mentioned earlier), but also in more informal ways, through routine cultural practices and in the daily talk of ordinary people, as they reveal the complexities, contradictions, and passions of what this identity means to them as situated individuals and groups.

Thus it is clear that political narratives have a significant role to play in realising social change. They help to establish the framework through which communities make sense of themselves, and their dynamic nature is such that, as many have commented, the past is never really past, for different versions of the past invariably arise in different times and places. As Dienstag comments

> Debates over the meaning of history cannot be exorcised from politics...Whoever abandons work on memory to others may find themselves imprisoned by the results...Human beings fight over history because they conceive their pasts to be an essential part of who they are. And they are right.[28]

If political narratives invariably change over time, and they do, how is it that this happens? To return to my original question, why is it that Obama has been able to inject new meaning into the American national narrative? (Garrison Keillor commented that on November 5th, 2008, the world awoke to find many Americans no longer feeling that they had to pretend to be Canadian.) There are certain key features which were instrumental in Obama's successful re-invention of what it means to be American. These include: (1) the compelling manner in which he recounts his own personal biography; (2) the way in which he relates his story to a more generic 'American story'; (3) his explicit collection of and reliance upon other personal narratives; and (4) the connections he makes between present-day and historical narratives.

'OUT OF ONE, MANY . . . ': OBAMA'S UNUSUAL AMERICAN ODYSSEY

Although virtually all politicians tell stories about themselves, their backgrounds, their communities, their roots, and their personal struggles, Obama is unusual in the extent to which he explicitly and continuously refers to his own biography, and the skilful way in which he interweaves it with a broader theme, that of 'the American story'. In the opening words of his address to the Democratic convention in 2004—a speech which in the eyes of many placed him for the first time in centre stage of American politics—he began by saying,

> Let's face it, my presence on this stage is pretty unlikely. My father was a foreign student, born and raised in a small village in Kenya. He grew up herding goats, went to school in a tin-roof shack.[29] His father—my grandfather—was a cook, a domestic servant to the British.... [My mother] was born in a town on the other

side of the world, in Kansas...My parents shared not only an improbable love, they shared an abiding faith in the possibilities of this nation....And I stand here today, grateful for the diversity of my heritage,....I stand here knowing that my story is part of the larger American story, that I owe a debt to all of those who came before me, and that, in no other country on earth, is my story even possible.[30]

Throughout his political career, Obama has made references to 'his funny name'. In 2006, he described his experiences when he first ran for state senate. He said when he approached people in 'barber shops, bake sales, guys standing on the corner' he was always met by the question:

Where'd you get that funny name, Barack Obama? Because people just couldn't pronounce it. They'd call me "Alabama", or they'd call me "Yo Mama". And I'd have to explain that I got the name from my father, who was from Kenya.[31]

Schama summarises the many strands of Obama's biography:

Through Barack Hussein Obama runs culture lines that connect Kenya with Kansas; ethnically complicated Polynesian-Asian Hawaii with black south Chicago; Scots-Irish bloodlines with a touch of Cherokee on his maternal grandmother's side. His and Michelle's daughters, Malia and Sasha, bring together west and east Africa; the atrocity of the slave ships with his Luo father's voluntary immigration.[32]

Such is the power of his particular biography that in the words of Cobb (2010), he is 'freighted with the vast weight of his own symbolism....a metaphor for a metaphor. It is possible, almost unavoidable, to see Obama's entire life—from birth to inauguration—as a referendum on civil rights causes'.[33]

In the comparatively short time that Obama has been on the international political scene, his personal story has become familiar to much of the world; indeed it is hard to remember that there was a time when many did not, in fact, know how to pronounce his name.[34] In November 2008, the month of the U.S. presidential election, his two autobiographical memoirs *Dreams from My Father* and *Audacity to Hope* were ranked number one and number two on the *New York Times* bestseller list[35] (rankings which were also shared across the Atlantic, on the *Observer*'s non-fiction UK paperback bestseller list).[36] Obama's personal voyage to the White House has become so well known that many of us felt a personal warmth to see the various members of his family—'brothers, sisters, nieces, nepthews, uncles and cousins, of every race and every hue, scattered across three continents' as he described them in what has now become known as his 'race' speech—gathered in Washington to celebrate, with what seemed like the rest of the world, the first inauguration of this not 'most conventional candidate' realising his 'improbable quest'. There was Auma, and Obongo, and Maya, and even Granny Sarah, nearly 90 years old. And two days before the election, when his grandmother Madelyn Dunham ('Toot') died, the nation joined Obama in mourning her death.[37] We knew them, even if they didn't know us.

Obama had a story to tell, and he told it well.[38] In the eyes of Toni Morrison, one of the most skilled wordsmiths of our times, Obama is 'a writer in my high esteem'. In an interview with National Public Radio, Morrison remarked on Obama's

> ability to reflect on this extraordinary mesh of experiences that he has had, some familiar and some not, and to really meditate on that the way he does, and to set up scenes in narrative structure, dialogue, conversation—all of these things that you don't often see, obviously, in the routine political memoir biography. [. ..] It's unique. It's his. There are no other ones like that.[39]

But Obama is much more than a gifted storyteller. No matter how mesmerising his accounts of life in Kisumu, Chicago's Southside, Honolulu and Jakarta may have been, what was special about Obama's stories is that they represent so much more than his own individual life, a personal narrative which symbolises Blake's 'a world in a grain of sand'. In the speech he made in Philadelphia on March 18, 2008, he describes his story as 'a story that has seared into my genetic makeup the idea that this nation is more than the sum of its parts—that out of many, we are truly one'. Equally, however, Obama embodies the quintessentially American narrative of diversity. Cobb writes: 'The American creed of "Out of many, one" has been turned on its head, a character defined by the ideal of "Out of one, many"'.[40]

Obama's personal story of his roots becomes transformed into so much more when it is woven into the wider narrative of what it means to be American. Hannah Arendt comments that:

> even the greatest forces of intimate life—passions of the heart, the thoughts of the mind, the delights of the senses—lead to an uncertain, shadowy kind of existence unless and until they are transformed, deprivatized and deindividualized, as it were, into a shape to fit them for public appearance. The most current of such transformations occurs in storytelling.[41]

Dreams from My Father meets this challenge of the de-individualisation of personal narrative masterfully, doing justice to both the unique and broader aspects of his own experiences.

For Obama, the flow between micro and macro narratives is two-way; not only does he connect his personal journey to a wider American narrative, but equally, in the larger plotline, he sees himself and the journey he and others have travelled. In *Dreams from My Father*, he describes his attraction to biblical stories—a passage which he himself quoted in his 'More Perfect Union' (a.k.a. 'race') speech:

> Those stories—of survival, and freedom, and hope—became our story, my story; the blood that had spilled was our blood, the tears our tears...Our trials and triumphs became at once unique and universal, black and more than black...[42]

Here, and elsewhere, Obama travels subtlely and—politically speaking—significantly between an 'I' and a 'we'. He manages to establish an important relationship between himself and others, his story and theirs, linking his narrative not only to others in the present day, but also to an enduring narrative which stretches across time, and is the lifeblood of the nation.

THE GREAT EMANCIPATOR AND THE BROTHER-IN-CHIEF[43]

That Obama has publicly pointed to Abraham Lincoln as something like a personal mentor cannot escape even the most casual of political observers. If one had missed articles such as the one which appeared in *Time* magazine in 2005 entitled 'What I See in Lincoln's Eyes', it still would have been difficult not to notice the symbolism of Lincoln at critical points in the campaign, and finally—and theatrically—throughout his first inauguration and the days leading up to it. And it was only fitting that Obama should become president in the bi-centenary year of Lincoln's birth.

Like Lincoln, Obama stepped onto the stage of national politics as the junior senator from Illinois. Obama has spoken of Lincoln's 'humble beginnings, which often speak to my own' and says that 'it was hard to imagine a less likely scenario' that he would win his race for the Senate, 'except, perhaps, for the one that allowed a child born in the backwoods of Kentucky with less than a year of formal education to end up as Illinois' greatest citizen and our nation's greatest President'.[44] Given the affinity which Obama has expressed for Lincoln, it is not altogether surprising that he announced his candidacy for president in Springfield, Illinois, on the steps of the Old Capitol, where Lincoln had practiced law, and where he delivered his

Figure 5.1:
Obama's presidential campaign inspired many articles. Ron English's 'Abraham Obama' become an iconic image of Obama's 2008 election campaign.

famous 'A House Divided' speech. In 2009 when Obama travelled with his family to Washington, DC to attend his presidential inauguration, he did so by boarding a train in Philadelphia, and following the historic route which Lincoln took to his own inauguration. The concert which officially kicked off the celebrations of the inauguration was held at the Lincoln Memorial. In his brief address on that bitter cold Sunday afternoon, as more than a million people gathered on the mall to welcome their new president and to listen to some of the greatest bands of our times, Obama told the crowds '...behind me, watching over the union he saved, sits the man who in so many ways made this day possible'.[45] And again, a few weeks later, speaking in the Capitol on the bicentenary of Lincoln's birth, Obama expressed 'a special gratitude to this singular figure who in so many ways made my own story possible—and who in so many ways made America's story possible'.[46]

At the inaugural swearing-in ceremony, Obama used the same actual Bible which Lincoln himself used to be sworn in as the 16th president of the nation in 1861—something which no other president has done.[47] And at the luncheon following the swearing in, Obama chose one of Lincoln's favourite meals (seafood, game, and root vegetables) which was served on replicas of Lincoln's White House china.

All this conscious mirroring notwithstanding, however, it is important to consider that it is, in Obama's words, 'the man and not the icon that speaks to me'. He then elaborates on this view:

I cannot swallow whole the view of Lincoln as the Great Emancipator. As a law professor and civil rights lawyer and as an African American, I am fully aware of his limited views on race. Anyone who actually reads the Emancipation Proclamation knows it was more a military document than a clarion call for justice... But it is precisely those imperfections—and the painful self-awareness of those failings etched in every crease of his face and reflected in those haunted eyes—that make him so compelling.[48]

It is Lincoln the man,[49] with all his imperfections and contradictions, to whom Obama is drawn. Lincoln not only reminds Obama of his own struggles, but 'he also reminded me of a larger, fundamental element of American life—the enduring belief that we can constantly remake ourselves to fit our larger dreams'. Moreover, he adds, 'as we remake ourselves, we remake our surroundings'.[50] Remaking ourselves, re-inventing who we are and what we stand for, is what Obama is all about. He places himself in the shadow of Lincoln's narrative precisely because that narrative is so open for interpretation, full of contradictions, and enduring.

Francesca Polletta (2006) argues convincingly that one of the most important criteria for effective strategic use of political narratives is their ability to mean different things to different people. Stories, Polletta suggests, 'may be influential precisely insofar as they are open to multiple interpretations',[51] and, again, stories are 'effective in fostering agreement across difference, not in spite of their normative ambiguity but because of it'.[52] Lincoln is a figure who can simultaneously hold contradictory positions. Lincoln's memory has long served the function of 'unifying opposites', as Barry Schwartz's work has well documented. He is both the common man who split logs, and the man carved out of white marble. Lincoln, Schwartz writes, 'became America's universal man: changing and remaining the same; standing beside the people and above the people; a reflection of and model for them—at once behind, above, and within them'.[53] Schwartz's work documents the changing fortunes of Lincoln's reputation, and argues that it was not until the Progressive Movement, at the beginning of the 20th century, that he began to assume the shape of 'a god in human form'.[54] The reason he gives for this advance in reputation relates directly to Obama's comment earlier, that we remake ourselves to fit our larger dreams. As we remake ourselves, we remould our models as well. The past is never past, but is always constructed in service of the needs of the present:

Lincoln was not elevated at the time because the people had discovered new facts about him, but because they had discovered new facts about themselves, and regarded him as the perfect vehicle for giving these tangible expression.... The reconstruction of Abraham Lincoln during the Progressive Era was the making of a complex figure, one whose contradictory qualities reproduced the contradictions of American society. Elevating Lincoln, the Americans affirmed for themselves their commitment to both commonness and greatness.[55]

It is Lincoln's memory as it serves the needs of the present which is key to understanding why his figure cuts such an attractive model for Obama's message. Speaking on the 200th anniversary of Lincoln's birth, in Springfield, Illinois, Obama described Lincoln as a man who:

> ... knew, better than anyone, what it meant to pull yourself up by your bootstraps. He understood that strain of personal liberty and self-reliance at the heart of the American experience. But he also understood something else. He recognized that while each of us must do our part, work as hard as we can, and be as responsible as we can—in the end, there are certain things we cannot do on our own. There are certain things we can only do together. There are certain things only a union can do.[56]

And at this point, evoking the memory of Lincoln, Obama delivers a speech about the current economic crisis, and what must be done to fight it.

> Only a nation can do these things. Only by coming together, all of us, and expressing that sense of shared sacrifice and responsibility—for ourselves and one another—can we do the work that must be done in this country. That is the definition of being American.... We will be remembered for what we choose to make of this moment. And when posterity looks back on our time, as we are looking back on Lincoln's, I don't want it said that we saw an economic crisis, but did not stem it... That we were consumed with small things when we were called to do great things. Instead, let them say that this generation—our generation—of Americans rose to the moment and gave America a new birth of freedom and opportunity in our time.[57]

Here one can see clearly Obama's most skillful use of political narratives. While honoring Lincoln—a man who 'rose to the moment' during a national crisis—he manages to breathe new life into an old story. His sense of narrative timing is brought to the fore as he asks his audience to project their imaginations into the future, and think how we as a nation might look back on actions we now take, or fail to take. Like Lincoln, 'we will be remembered for what we choose to make of this moment'.

Schwartz argues that the debates regarding the nature of collective memory—Is it essentially continuous or discontinuous?—are resolved 'nowhere more clearly and more dramatically than in America's memory of Abraham Lincoln'.[58] It is, Schwartz argues, both. There is a general sense in which Lincoln's legacy endures—albeit in different manifestations—since his death in 1864. But equally, what and how he is remembered, and for what purpose, are questions which each generation must answer anew. And so, as we see in Obama's speech marking the anniversary of his birth, we are presented with Abe the log-splitter, Abe the man who did not shirk from making difficult decisions, whose memory is placed in the context of the current world economic crisis.

The Lincoln industry has been a long and thriving one—and as Schwartz and others have commented, the construction of him as a man and as a politician has had many and varied forms in the 150 years since his death. Still, it is probably more than a coincidence that it is particularly flourishing at the same time as Obama's presidency. Adam Gopnik, himself a biographer of Lincoln, refers to the new Lincoln literature as 'multiplying by fission, as amoebas do, on the airport bookstore shelves'.[59] In November 2012, American History Professor James McPherson published an article in the *The New York Review of Books* in which he reviewed four recent books on Lincoln. At roughly the same time, two Lincoln films—of rather different genres—had been launched on both sides of the Atlantic. *Abraham Lincoln: Vampire Hunter* casts our hero in conflict with vampires who are planning to take over the United States. *Lincoln* is Steven Spielberg's attempt to tell the iconic story of Lincoln's attempt to pass the 13th Amendment. In the first two weeks after its release, it had taken in $62 million at the box office—almost as much as it cost to make it. A review of the movie, written a few days after its release and the week after the presidential election in November 2012, remarks: '...for a few days or weeks now, it *is* the moment in a way few modern movies have managed. It's very good, but that's not the point. It's necessary'.[60] There are many lessons for our time to be taken from the movie, not least that second terms in the White House are not always easy. Days after his re-election, Obama watched the film with Spielberg and many members of the case, including Daniel Day Lewis (who would later get the Oscar for his performance), at a special screening at the White House. Obama explained the 'incredibly powerful' effect that the film had on him:

> What made [Lincoln] such a remarkable individual, as well as a remarkable President, was his capacity to balance the idea that there are some eternal truths with the fact that we live in the here and now, and the here and now is messy and difficult. And anything we do is going to be somewhat imperfect. And so what we try to do is just tack in the right direction... Being able to project across

a very long timeline while still being focused on the immediate tug and pull of politics I think is a useful lesson, and an accurate portrayal of how I think about my work day to day.[61]

Gopnik sees a different cautionary tale. Lincoln, far from embracing the spirit of conciliation, was effective because he was willing to fight his enemies. As he writes: 'When the South seceded, Lincoln chose war—an all-out, brutal, bitter war of a kind that had never been fought until then. "Let the erring sisters go in peace"! the editor Horace Greeley recommended, and Lincoln said, "Lock the doors and make them stay"'.[62] Needless to say, there is much in the story of Lincoln for those of us in these troubled modern times to contemplate.

RIPPLES OF HOPE

Despite—or maybe even because of—being steeped in American history, Obama is driven by an intention to shift the national narrative. He has been very forthright in his condemnation of the way in which a very particular, and narrow, construction of what it means to be American has come to dominate American politics. In his 2009 inaugural speech, he drew a clear line under the reign of the previous administration: 'We reject as false the choice between our safety and our ideals'. In the words of one commentator, 'the story Obama gave the American people, and the world, is as old as the hills: "the king is dead. Long live the king"'.[63]

He has insisted throughout his time in the public light that we need not only more stories, but more kinds of stories, reflecting the many varied walks of life. In his 'race speech', which marked a pivotal turning point in his campaign, he spoke of 'the racial stalemate we've been stuck in for years'. He criticised Jeremiah Wright not for speaking about the racism which is endemic in American life, but rather for speaking 'as if our society was static'. Just as Obama had chosen the steps of the Springfield Old Town Hall to launch his bid for presidency, so his choice of place for this difficult speech was made with care. Obama delivered his speech in the heart of old Philadelphia, just two blocks from the Liberty Bell and Independence Hall. And he opened by referring to principles upon which the nation had been founded, and said that the challenge to build 'a more perfect union' was still ongoing: 'we cannot solve the challenges of our time unless we solve them together—unless we perfect our union by understanding that we may have different stories, but we hold common hopes'.[64] The speech which Obama made on that day was a passionate plea against conducting business as usual. 'Not this time' he told the crowds again and again. This time we want to talk about something different. We want our lives, and those of our fellow citizens, to be different. This time we are moving on. Nowhere can one find a more dramatic illustration of Obama's master narrative of change, based on a continuity with the principles upon which the country was founded. Obama's defense of gay marriage has been framed in a similar way. 'Our journey is not complete until our gay brothers and sisters are treated like anyone else under the law. For if we are truly created equal, then surely the love we commit to one another must be equal as well',[65] he proclaimed in his second inaugural speech. Rather than depicting gay marriage as something new, instead he places it within the age-old story of the fight for equality.

This strategy of encasing a call for change within an affirmation of a continuity of principle is one which Obama had used to similar effect in his speech at the Democratic Convention in 2004. During this speech, Obama firmly located his message within the framework of the founding narratives of the nation. 'We hold these truths to be self evident' he told the crowds. And then he made the opening lines of the Declaration of Independence as fresh and as poignant as if they had been written by him, addressing the most urgent issues of the day. 'This year, in this election we are called to reaffirm our values and our commitments, to hold them against a hard reality and see how we're measuring up to the legacy of our forbearers and the promise of future generations'.[66] One of the most interesting things Obama did during this rousing speech is that he began to reappropriate the national narrative. The Bush Administration, for all their talk about patriotism and their hunt for anti-American activity within its own shores, had forgotten the key master narrative, the founding principles of the country. Obama was asking of the American people to 'see how we were measuring up to our legacy'.[67] He would dust off the old words and phrases that everyone knew but which had somehow become hallow, and he would breathe new life into them. And in the process, he would lay new claim to those principles.

'E pluribus unum: "Out of many, one."' It seemed like those words as Obama spoke them on that July night in 2004 had come to mean something new. He continued.

> ... there is not a liberal America and a conservative America—there is the United States of America. There is not a Black America and a White America and Latino America and Asian America—there's the United States of America.
>
> The pundits, the pundits like to slice-and-dice our country into Red States and Blue States; Red States for Republicans, Blue States for Democrats. But I've

Figure 5.2:
'Fifty States One Union' echoes Obama's rhetoric of a unified America.

got news for them, too. We worship an "awesome God" in the Blue States, and we don't like federal agents poking around in our libraries in the Red States. We coach Little League in the Blue States and yes, we've got some gay friends in the Red States. There are patriots who opposed the war in Iraq and there are patriots who supported the war in Iraq. We are one people, all of us pledging allegiance to the stars and stripes, all of us defending the United States of America.[68,69]

Obama rejects the traditional storyline; he complicates the narrative, instilling in it multiple voices which nonetheless join together under one stars and stripes.

Obama has stayed on message for many years—something which has been observed by many, including those he worked with in days of his community organising on Chicago's Southside. And his message, which he framed in terms of hope and change, all came back to this simple belief which combines a respect for difference ('out of many') with a belief in the possibility of working together, unity ('one'): E pluribus unum.

On Election Day, November 4, 2009, it came to pass that more people from more walks of life felt that they had something to vote for than has ever happened in the history of the United States. More votes were cast in this election than had been cast in any other U.S. presidential election. Approximately 131.2 million people voted. In terms of the percentage of eligible voters, this meant that the voter turnout rate was approximately

63 percent, or the highest since 1960, and the third highest since women began voting.[70] Comparing the 2008 election to the election of 2004, which was itself notable for a high voter turnout, interesting patterns emerge. Although there was a decrease in voting by whites, nearly 3 million more African-Americans voted than in 2004 (an increase of 21%), Latino votes rose by 16 percent (more than 1.5 million), and young Americans (aged 18–29) cast 1.8 million more votes, or a 9 percent increase.[71]

Despite many predictions to the contrary, the numbers were not hugely different in the election of 2012, and what followed in its wake was much political commentary on the changing face of American demographics. What this means is not only that there were more people who could recognise themselves and their lives in the multivocal narrative which Obama offered them, but that they could come together, as different as their backgrounds might be, and put him in the White House, not once, but twice. This is why, in his Election Night victory speech in 2008, he told the crowds that for those who had doubts about the power of American democracy, the results of that night were their answer:

> It's the answer told by lines that stretched around schools and churches in numbers this nation has never seen; by people who waited three hours and four hours, many for the very first time in their lives, because they believed that this time must be different; that their voice could be that difference. It's the answer spoken by young and old, rich and poor, Democrat and Republican, black, white, Latino, Asian, Native American, gay, straight, disabled and not disabled—Americans who sent a message to the world that we have never been a collection of Red States and Blues States: we are, and always will be, the United States of America.[72]

He told the crowds 'This is your victory' and he was right. On the morning of November 5, 2008, the *New York Times* ran a headline announcing Obama's victory in 96-point type. 'Only three events in the paper's history—the Apollo landing, Richard Nixon's resignation, and September 11 attacks—were heralded with equal dimensions'.[73]

But change did not come to Washington as quickly as many had hoped it would. Indeed, after four years in the White House, many of those who had been Obama's most ardent supporters felt that their dreams had been far from realised. Some of the blame for this lay beyond Obama—even the president of the United States could not be held responsible for the global financial collapse. But there were other things which made people feel that the rhetoric of change fell far short of the reality.[74] In some sense this feeling of disappointment was inevitable. As Frank Rich comments:

Of course Barack Obama was too hot not to cool down. He was the one so many were waiting for—not only the first African-American president but also the nation's long-awaited liberator after eight years of Bush-Cheney, the golden-tongued evangelist who could at long last revive and sell the old liberal faith, the first American president in memory to speak to voters as if they might be thinking adults, the first national politician in years to electrify the young. He was even, of all implausible oddities, a contemporary politician-author who actually wrote his own books. The Obama of Hope and Change was too tough an act for Obama, a mere chief executive, to follow.[75]

Other commentators feel that Obama's accomplishments in office have been underappreciated—'an underappreciation that is as pronounced as the overestimation in those heady early days'.[76]

In the run-up to the 2012 election, the Republicans adopted a strategy to make the electorate feel 'that they'd taken part in a noble failure'.[77] The *New York Times* reported on Ryan's speech to the Republican National Convention: 'College graduates should not have to live out their 20s in their childhood bedrooms, staring up at fading Obama posters and wondering when they can move out and get going with life', he said midway through his speech, eliciting laughter and delighted applause.[78] And yet, as blogger Amy Davidson wrote on the night of Obama's re-election: '...some things hadn't faded, it turned out. Obama won, and will still be the president when Malia is old enough to vote for his successor'.[79]

The Republicans were right about something, though. The biggest challenge to Obama's re-election was not Mitt Romney, but 'the ghost of Barack Obama 2008'.[80] No one was more aware of this than Obama himself, who acknowledged the frustration that people were feeling with the rate of change.

A number of commentators noted that securing his re-election helped Barack Obama to find his voice again. (In the weeks leading up to the election he had also, literally, lost his voice). The day after the election, Jon Stewart asked 'Is that all he needed, the knowledge that he would never ever have to run for office again'? Although the conservative press described his victory speech in Chicago as 'far less hopey-changey than his rockstar delivery four years ago',[81] others found it 'better than anything we've heard from him for a long while'.[82]

The day following his re-election, Obama made a visit to the Chicago headquarters of his campaign, where he spoke with volunteers. He had come to thank them for everything. Again, he returned to his own biography.

"So...you guys," President Obama began, as he stood in a room that looks, in a video his campaign released yesterday evening, like it had seen the wear of long nights and pizza boxes.... Obama talked about when he first moved to Chicago, wanting to change the world. "I didn't really know how to do it," he said. He got a job as a community organizer, and learned something, he said, about aspirations, as well as needs. "It taught me something about how I handle disappointment, and to what it meant to work hard on a common endeavor. And I grew up. I became a man during that process," he said. And so when I come here, and I look at all of you, what comes to mind is, is not actually that you guys remind me of myself, it's the fact that you are so much better than I was. In so many ways. You're smarter. You're better organized. And, um, you, you're more effective. And so I am absolutely confident that all of you are going to do just amazing things in your lives. And what Bobby Kennedy called the ripples of hope[83] that come out when you throw a stone in the lake—that's going to be *you*.... And that's why even before last night's results I felt that the work that I had done, in running for office, had come full circle. Because what you guys have done proves that the work that I'm doing is important. I'm really proud of that. I'm really proud of all of you.[84]

Exhausted, and wiping away his tears, we hear Obama once again connecting his biography to that of others, and to the winds of change in American history. As his once colleague at Harvard Law School and now biographer James Kloppenberg comments: 'Change in a democracy is a work of decades, not months or even years'.[85]

THE PLURALITY OF THE NARRATIVE

Throughout his campaign Obama appeared as one who represented the spirit of his times,[86] bringing to mind the historian E. H. Carr's classic description of 'a great man' [sic] of history as 'an outstanding individual who is at once a product and an agent of the historical process, at once the representative and the creator of social forces which change the shape of the world and the thoughts of men'.[87] Obama, 'a product and agent of the historical processes' continuously insisted that it is only through collective action that change can be realised. As he told those gathered to commemorate Lincoln's date of birth: 'There are certain things we can only do together. There are certain things only a union can do'.[88] It was not a rhetorical gesture which led him on election night 2008 to say to the thousands gathered in Grant Park that this was their victory. This message he continued in his sobering inaugural speech: 'Starting today, we must pick ourselves up, dust ourselves off, and begin again the work of remaking America'.[89] That Lincoln needed the nation in order to be a great man, does not diminish Lincoln's greatness.

Schama comments on the intersection of Obama's tenure as president and the fateful global economic crisis:

> There is no point asking whether Obama would have made it were the times not so out of whack. History made him and he made history... It has already been said that it's Obama's misfortune to be the first African-American president at a time of acute national crisis. But you can bet he doesn't see it that way; rather as the gift of challenge. Sometimes—as in 1860 with Abraham Lincoln and 1932 with Franklin D Roosevelt—the man and the moment do meet. This is one of those occasions.[90]

Earlier, I discussed the importance of political narratives for realising social change. The new version of the old story which Obama is putting before the American people is that these are hard times, and there is work to be done. Change will come, but only if we make it happen. His message is one of agency. '... there is nothing so satisfying to the spirit, so defining of our [national] character, than giving our all to a difficult task'.[91] he told the crowd of two million strong at his 2009 inauguration. Americans are people who 'do not grudgingly accept but rather seize gladly' our responsibilities and our duties. We are people who get things done. Whether it be the rugged pioneer spirit which settled the Wild West, or the sense of exploration which led to the moon, Americans revel in meeting hard challenges. Echoing the words that Martin Luther King told the crowds on April 3, 1968, the night before he died,[92] Obama told his supporters on election night 2009:

> The road ahead will be long. Our climb will be steep. We may not get there in one year or even one term, but America—I have never been more hopeful than I am tonight that we will get there. I promise you—we as a people will get there.[93]

Just how long the road would be, or how hard the climb, many—perhaps even including Obama—did not, and maybe even could not know. His appeal was not just eloquent, nor only full of historical resonance. In his 2009 inaugural address, Obama warned the people: 'the challenges we face are real. They are serious and they are many. The will not be met easily or in a short span of time. But know this, America—they will be met'.[94] Obama then closed this speech with Thomas Paine's account of George Washington leading his army across the Delaware River. From here he concluded: 'Let it be said by our children's children that when we were tested we... did not turn back and we did not falter'.[95] Obama's narrative has a temporal fluidity which makes its effect that much more powerful. It is a classical tale; the principles upon which our country was founded were right-minded; over the past 200 years, we have worked, and continue to work, at perfecting that union; sometimes we have lost our way; the business of America is to remake itself, to renew its commitment to those founding principles, and, with courage, to face the challenges ahead. 'The time has come' Obama said, 'to reaffirm our enduring sprit; to choose our better history'[96,97] The urgent call for renewal, and a demand for the commitment which it entails, was the central message of Obama's 'brave and surprising'.[98] inaugural address.

Obama's insistence on the importance of locating his personal narrative within a wider, collective narrative can also be seen in the concerted effort he made to include key civil rights activists of earlier generations in the inaugural celebrations, for instance by inviting all of the surviving members of the Little Rock Nine and the Tuskegee Airmen.[99] Melba Patillo Beals, one of the Little Rock Nine, commented that 'I think the stage will be shared with the ghosts of Martin Luther King, Jr., and Rosa Parks and (Mohandas) Ghandi...We all stand up on each other's shoulders....'[100] Beals continued: 'I'm honoured that Barack Obama saw fit to invite me. He has said that he aspired to climb the steps of the White House because the Little Rock Nine climbed the steps of Central High School'.[101] What was enacted on January 20, 2009 was a realisation of more than one man's journey from humble origins to the White House; it was a political narrative of social change.

THE QUEEN OF SOUL IS JUST ONE OF US

The day after Obama's 2009 inauguration, Larry King interviewed Aretha Franklin, asking her how she had felt about her performance the day before, singing in the presence of two million people, with the eyes of the world upon her. With the temperatures well below freezing, she explained 'Mother Nature was not very kind to me. I'm going to deal with her when I get home. It, by no means, was my standard. I was not happy with it'. This was amazing to me. Although I was impressed by her professionalism, I was struck by the fact that this critique was directed towards a moment I had already come to cherish. Standing in that crowd, hearing her sing, being part of that day, I realised that something had changed deep inside of me. I did not know that 'My Country Tis of Thee' could actually bring tears to my eyes; and even now, I find watching the video of that footage very moving. On that freezing cold day, the feeling of so much of the crowd was that finally we were beginning to thaw. This song, once sung by Marion Anderson on the steps of the Lincoln Memorial, had, in its past, heralded in a new day, and it was doing it

Figure 5.3:
The famous hat. Aretha described the inauguration as 'the promise of tomorrow coming to pass'.

again. We were re-inventing ourselves—a concept which is itself tied to the American national narrative about who we are.

Aretha might not have been pleased with her singing, but she felt the same way as most of us who were witnesses to that day. She finishes her interview by saying: 'I was delighted and thrilled to be there. That was the most important thing, not so much the performance, but just to be there and to see this great man go into office—the promise of tomorrow coming to pass'.[102]

When I told people that I intended to go to Washington for the inauguration, some of them asked me if I thought I would be able to 'see anything.' Like most of the two million who attended the inauguration, I didn't have tickets for the swearing-in ceremony, but what I saw on that day was far more than I could have ever imagined. I watched Obama take the oath of president from the steps of the Lincoln Memorial, about a mile walk along the river from where I was staying. The streets of downtown Washington were pedestrianised, and everywhere one went, people were walking in the streets, smiles on their faces, the bitter cold notwithstanding. Moments before the actual inauguration began, I realised my son had become separated from us. Other family members joined me in a frantic search for him—which lasted only ten minutes but felt like an eternity. By time we found him, he had already met some kind strangers, one of whom had placed him atop his shoulders, so he could look around and try to find us. The man standing next to me during the inauguration told me how he wished his father could have lived to see this day, and, both arms stretched up towards the sky, he wept as Obama was sworn in. When the crowd began to disperse at the end of the ceremonies, we hugged long and hard. And

Figure 5.4:
Obama 2009 inauguration taken from space.

at the parade that afternoon, we stood next to a man who kept shouting 'Pinch me, pinch me, I don't believe what I'm seeing'. When I went to have a drink with my dad the next night in a nearby bar, Aretha Franklin was at the next table. And all of us, Aretha, me, the man upon whose shoulders my son was perched, the friend I had made in the crowd, all of us, as different as we were, were there, celebrating the remaking of our national narrative.

Four years later, Michelle Obama, spoke to a crowd in Des Moines, Iowa, the last stop on the campaign trail before the 2012 election:

> Tomorrow, all across this state, all across this country, we will line up and vote in libraries and community centers, in school gyms.... while we have come so far, we know that there is so much more to do. And what we really, truly know is that we cannot turn back now. We need to keep moving this country forward.[103]

A tearful and hoarse Barack Obama then addressed the crowd, in his last ever appeal as a candidate for elected office:

> You took this campaign and you made it your own. And you organized your-selves, block by block, neighborhood by neighborhood, county by county, start-ing a movement that spread across the country, a movement made up of young

and old, and rich and poor, and black and white, Latino, Asian, Native American, gay, straight, Democrats, Republicans, who believe we've all got something to contribute; that we all deserve a shot at our own American Dream.[104]

Obama has continued throughout his time in public life to insist on a national identity which incorporates many different kinds of narratives. While embracing the importance of personal storylines, as varied as they made be, it is what we bring to the common good which lifts us beyond our own limited worlds: 'We've all got something to contribute'. It is the careful movement between the personal and public, between times past and what is to come, that makes Obama's political narrative so powerful.

One month into being a U.S. Senator, Barack Obama spoke to a group of people, gathered to mark the birthday of Civil Rights veteran John Lewis.[105] He began by quoting the words that Martin Luther King, Jr. had told a crowd of thousands after the Selma March had reached Montgomery:

> [Quoting King:] "The arc of the moral universe is long, but it bends towards justice." He's right, but you know what? It doesn't bend on its own. It bends because we help it bend that way. Because people like John Lewis and Hosea William and Martin Luther King and Coretta Scott King and Rosa Parks and thousands of ordinary Americans with extraordinary courage have helped bend it that way. And as their examples call out to us from across the generations, we continue to progress as a people because they inspire us to take our own two hands and bend that arc.[106]

The imagery of the arc invites us back into the realm of the narrative imagination. In order to realize social change, we must have a vision of a better alternative. But change only comes about when we align our imagination with our actions in the here and now.

Conclusion

I began this book with a discussion about ways in which narrative and imagination are integrally bound to one another in everyday life. In these pages, this linkage has been explored in a wide variety of ways: the sawing up of Christabel Pankhurst in magic tricks performed in the early 20th century; a 70-year-old grandmother discovering her talents as a rock-n'-roll DJ; Cicero's love of gardening; beauty salons in the American Midwest; the classroom of School Molly; and the revitalized American narrative, embodied by Aretha Franklin and the other two million people who attended Obama's inauguration in 2009. In all of these examples, and more, I have explored the connection between everyday experiences and their extension into what Sartre has called 'the not yet'. Reality is always narratively constructed; that is to say, it is grounded in temporality. How one perceives the present, that is, what is 'really there', is always and inevitably bound up with a construction of the past, with one eye to the future. These constructions are not fixed, but are forever in flux. Our imaginations, which reflect our own situatedness, play a significant role in which pieces of past experiences we bring together, how we assemble them to make sense of our present condition, and what we reach towards in the future.

Brockmeier (2009) has argued that there are three basic features of meanings; they are (1) relational; (2) societal and historical; and (3) indicate a range of possibilities for action (222). The implications of this tripartite anatomy of meaning are profound.

> Living in a world of cultural meanings means we have no choice but to choose: we must interpret them and make a decision about how to go about them, be it everyday issues like what to eat, or more momentous decisions like which

spouse and friends to live with and which life to live at all—which brings us back to the question of what meaning do we choose to give to our lives.[1]

The consideration of the role of imagination in everyday life is intricately bound to questions of our relationship to the world, to history, and to our ability to reflect upon our lives and to choose our actions. In this book, I have explored different ways in which these aspects of meaning making have been manifested in certain domains of everyday living. Ultimately, what Brockmeier suggests here is that the narrative imagination is intricately bound to questions of human agency; in 'creating novel meanings' the narrative imagination is capable of 'extending the symbolic space which a culture unfolds at a certain point in history, breaking through the limits of the materially given and transcending the horizon of physical causality'.[2] In this sense, our ability to locate a role for ourselves in the task of creating new realities rests with the narrative imagination—the bending of the arc of the moral universe, with our own two hands, as Obama described it in the last chapter.

Jules Cashford has commented that 'It is difficult to talk about the Imagination since we are by definition far from it when talk we *about* it' (Italics in the original).[3] Perhaps an academic book about imagination is not likely to yield as many rich offerings on this topic as a number of other entries into it, but my purpose in bringing imagination to the fore is as counterballast in the discussion of the narrative construction of reality. Without imagination, the meaning we attach to any given experience is by definition limited to what we already know. It is the narrative imagination which gives us the possibility of extending the boundaries of our worlds, as we have lived them and as they will hold us in the future.

TIME AND TIMELINESS

Andrew Motion, as he sat talking with 109-year-old Harry Patch,, spoke of his experience of time: 'The flow between "then" and "now" is unbroken'.[4] It is not that this temporal fluidity 'objectively' exists; rather it is something which is created in the mind of Motion, in that moment. Indeed, the theme of time and timeliness is one which has run throughout this book. Chapter 2 argued that the success of magic was in no small part dependent upon the context in which it was performed. Transporting the entirely fictional Indian rope trick to the land of the 'exotic' made it believable in the minds of many who, at that time, constructed India as place which bordered on the surreal. What we are prepared to 'believe', and how this affects all walks of our lives—including our scholarly research—has everything to do with the frameworks of meaning making which we have built in our minds.

The leap which is required to travel from the here and now to the world of different possibilities is one which challenges not only individuals, and social collectives, but also historical eras. That this is true, that each new generation is endowed with the responsibility—which is also a gift—to look anew at the world which they have been born into, is evident when one considers the trajectory of political narratives. Obama's rhetoric of change, and its particular revitalization of the narrative of what it means to be American, are framed within a re-construction of the principles upon which the country was founded. Although Obama's narrative is anchored in the past, its boundaries extend into the future; the past is used to reconstruct the present, with implications for building a new possible future. The timeliness of his message is a fundamental reason for its success. With his unusual biography and meteoric journey to the White House, he both made history, and history made him.

Questions of the perception of time, and its passage, are central to considerations of the meaning of age. Oftentimes, the stages of life are constructed as being discontinuous. When we are young, we are not socialized to think of the old people we will (hopefully) one day become. Equally, as we age, there is a tendency to speak of 'the young' as if they were a homogenous group who together constituted a world of the unknown, and perhaps unknowable. Rarely do we engage in cross-generational conversations about age, and this absence contributes to what Simon de Beauvoir has called 'the conspiracy of silence'.[5] The effects of this are detrimental not only to the old, but to everyone who is aging, that is to say everyone who is alive. It is for each of us, individually and together, to contemplate the meaning of age, as we live through the passing of time. This requires from us a nuanced sensitivity for balancing that which is familiar with that which is strange or unknown. Rebecca Solnit describes 'the journey between the near and the far in every life'. She continues:

> Sometimes an old photograph, an old friend, an old letter will remind you that you are not who you once were, for the person who dwelt among them, valued this, chose that, wrote thus, no longer exists. Without noticing it you have transversed a great distance; the strange has become familiar and the familiar if not strange at least awkward or uncomfortable, an outgrown garment.[6]

As we age, we invariably experience ourselves both as similar to, and quite different from, the selves we once were. Human development is indeed marked by this interplay between change and constancy, a holding on and letting go, selves always in the midst of being and in the process becoming.

It is the goal of education, philosopher Mary Warnock tells us, to instil in students 'the feeling of infinity', the sense that there is more to the world than the eye can see. In this sense, the narrative imagination might be said to be not only timely—relevant to the issues which confront students and teachers in their daily lives—but also timeless, transporting students to a place beyond the here and now. In order to engage in the world of ideas, students must have a sense that the worlds which they know are not only acknowledged but also valued by those who seek to teach them. It is difficult if not impossible to engage intellectually with a set of concepts which hold no apparent relevance to one's life. Preparing the ground for an environment in which learning is possible, teachers need to establish a connection between themselves, their own engagement with their discipline, and their students. This demands a recognition that all of us are learners; although teachers must be willing to lead and to mentor, they must be equally willing to listen and to absorb. Teachers, all of whom were once students, depend upon the success of learners for the future of scholarship. Each has her role to play within and beyond the classroom, but all are part of a cycle of knowledge.

IMAGINING DIFFERENCE

Narrative imagination is 'the means of sympathy' Denis Donoghue writes. It is, he says 'the capacity to imagine being different; to enter notionally and experimentally upon experiences we have not had, ways of life other than our own'.[7] Whether and how one can 'imagine difference' has been a discussion throughout this book.

The relationship between 'knowing thyself' and knowing others is one which has long attracted debate. In the Introduction, I discussed the works of Kapuściński and Levinas, who argue that self-knowledge is predicated upon knowledge of the other. Only another can act as a mirror for ourselves. This sentiment goes some way to explaining our passion for scholarship. Even while we want to learn about worlds which extend beyond our own, those explorations in turn teach us something about ourselves. Still, it is our challenge not to reduce all difference to a homogeneity which boils down to the world as we know it. What one finds believable and what one discards as improbable, if not impossible, are in some measure influenced by our own situatedness. But if we are to learn anything in our scholarly endeavors, we must entertain the possibility that life might be very different from the way in which we envision it. Other people's realities might vary greatly from our own, and if we take this seriously, we must remain open to having our expectations challenged. Ultimately, good research demands that an investigator is willing to make herself vulnerable. Suspending disbelief, we might learn something about another way of viewing life. In the process, we might learn something about ourselves as well.

'Of all realities [old age] is perhaps that of which we retain a purely abstract notion longest in our lives', Proust reflected.[8] Although, clearly, we do not know our own old age until we reach it, at the end of our lives, this sense of distance is also enhanced by age-regulatory systems which are built upon assumptions of difference between the life stages. In in-depth conversations I have had with people in their 8th, 9th and 10th decades of life,[9] I have heard time and again that the experience of growing old is characterized by a sense of change and constancy. As we grow older, we are both the same person we have always been, and yet also, different from that earlier self. But this is not unique to later life. Yes, our bodies change, and so do the things we can and can't do with them. Equally, relationships evolve, people are born, people die, we move house, change professions; but all of these markers happen across the life cycle. Throughout our days, life carries on, and our sense of who we are adapts to the changes we experience. Because we do not often contemplate the meaning of aging in our lives, we cannot imagine being any other age—it is as if we have never been young and will never be old. This is a failure of narrative imagination.

The classroom can be a place which brings together very different worlds. Not only does everyone—students and teachers alike—arrive with their cluster of life experiences, but the process of learning helps us to develop a reflexive perspective on those life worlds. According to Sartre, the ability to step back from our own situation and to envision non-actual situations is identical with the ability to imagine.[10] One of the key goals of education is to develop 'the aim of imaginative understanding'.[11] Similarly, Nussbaum argues that a primary function of education is to develop the narrative imagination of students. This 'muscle' is the means by which students make themselves vulnerable, opening themselves to understanding what life might feel like from the point of view of someone who is very different from themselves. This not only gives students perspective on their own lives, offering them an opportunity for greater reflection and understanding, but it also is a key ingredient for democratic citizenship—the recognition that I am but one amongst many, that each of us has our own perspectives, and that how we see things might from time to time clash. Through exercising our narrative imagination, we increase our awareness of the choices available to us. In this way, education which is built upon a recognition of difference has the potential to enhance our understanding of the world, and our sense of agency within it.

Obama's political narrative is built upon the bedrock of imagining difference. The author of two autobiographies before the age of 50, he is a man whose journey not only spans four continents, but the story he tells about himself is crafted to bring together—but not to erase—difference. From this personal story, he extends out to national narrative. Red States and Blue States. Black and White. Gay and Straight. Abled and Disabled. Americans all of them. 'We are, and always will be, the United States of America' he has said time and again. Both the principled simplicity and the practical complexity of this narrative render it so compelling for some, threatening for others. Conservative intellectual Dinesh D'Souza comments that Obama

spent his formative years—the first 17 years of his life—off the American mainland, in Hawaii, Indonesia and Pakistan, with multiple subsequent journeys to Africa. A good way to discern what motivates Obama is to ask a simple question: What is his dream? Is it the American dream? Is it Martin Luther King's dream? Or something else?[12]

The answer to his question is that 'we' (presumably those he regards as legitimate Americans), 'have been blinded to his real agenda because, across the political spectrum, we all seek to fit him into some version of American history'. Effectively, D'Souza is arguing that we have become intoxicated by our imaginations—and in doing so, we have become lost.

But maybe it is precisely being lost, or rather in Keats' words being capable of 'being in uncertainties, mysteries, doubts'[13] which we require. The experience of being lost can simply mean that

... the world has become larger than your knowledge of it... it is not, afterall, really a question about whether you can know the unknown, arrive in it, but how to go about looking for it, how to travel... Never to get lost is not to live".[14]

POSSIBLE LIVES

Jens Brockmeier (2009) has argued that 'the narrative imagination is pivotal in probing and extending real and fictive scenarios of agency'.[15] The ability to imagine, which is a key force behind our ability to create meaning, and multiple meanings, is integrally bound to how we live our lives, and our ability to discern other possible ways of being. In this sense, meaning is 'a possibility of action'.[16] Building on this notion, Brockmeier suggests that narrative imagination is 'a form and practice of human agency' allowing us to create alternative visions for our lives, and indeed our world. '[N]arratives are capable of extending the symbolic space which a culture unfolds in a certain point in history',[17] thus playing a vital role in the development of cultures over time.

Narrative imagination and everyday life is a topic which, by definition, seeps in to all corners of our existence, from the most mundane to the most abstract. Many different kinds of stories have filled these pages: personal stories (my own and others); magical stories; stories of learning; stories of aging; stories of political engagement; stories of the challenge of scholarship. Using these examples, I have analyzed the complex and multileveled ways that our imaginations are intimately tied to who we are and who we might be; in fact they are always with us, not only part of what we see in the present, but helping to carve time and again our understandings of the past and visions of the future. Our situated imaginations are the mechanism by which we connect our story to wider stories, the ligaments which run between the micro detail of our daily existence and the macro narrative of the movement of history. Through our narrative imagination, we are not alone, even when there is no one with us. It connects us always to others who are not there, including our past and future selves.

Ted Hughes writes:

> The outer world and inner world are interdependent at every moment. We are simply the locus of their collision. Two worlds, with mutually contradictory laws, or laws that seem to us to be so, colliding afresh at every second, struggling for peaceful co-existence. And whether we like it or not our life is what we are able to make out of that collision and struggle. So what we need, evidently, is a faculty that embraces both worlds simultaneously...and which pays equal respects to both sides...This really is Imagination.[18]

Here Hughes encapsulates the power of imagination, which is both grounded in the struggle of our everyday life and is at the same time the very mechanism which allows us to extend beyond what is already real. It is through our imaginations that we link our past, present, and possible futures. Poet Lawrence Sail points to what he calls 'the ultimate negativity', asking 'Can you imagine a world without the Imagination? [19] Such a condition would leave us unescapably nailed to life as we know it, unable to visualize other possible worlds. Ultimately, the world stripped of imagination would be one in which what it means to be human would be compromised. 'To live possible lives in possible worlds', Brockmeier writes, 'is inherent to the human condition... Real or imagined, narrated or enacted, discovered in one's past or projected into one's future, our possible lives are a constitutive part of our selves'.[20] The narrative imagination is thus both fundamentally embedded in our everyday existence, even as it lifts our focus to the world as it might become. As such, it is our most precious 'resource of Hope'.[21]

Contemplating the role of narrative imagination in everyday life brings us finally to the question of what it means to know our world. If we are to acquire an understanding about the meaning of our lives in the larger sense, we must have a way of moving beyond current reality, even while being anchored within it. If we can abandon our paths of certainty, and thus render ourselves vulnerable to new ways of knowing, we will not only be transformed in the process, but we can, in our small way, contribute towards creating new realities. This possibility of renewal and change is one of greatest gifts of our narrative imagination.

NOTES

Chapter 1

1. Brockmeier, Jens. 2009. "Reaching for Meaning: Human Agency and the Narrative Imagination." *Theory and Psychology* 19(2): 213–233.
2. Nussbaum, M. (1997) *Cultivating Humanity*. Cambridge, MA: Harvard University Press.
3. Brockmeier, Jens, "Reaching for Meaning," 213–233.
4. Salmon, Philida and Catherine Riessman. 2008. "Looking Back on Narrative Research: An Exchange." In *Doing Narrative Research*, edited by M. Andrews, C. Squire, and M. Tamboukou, p. 78. London: Sage.
5. Warnock, Mary. 1940/1972. "Introduction" to Jean Paul Sartre. *The Psychology of Imagination*. London: Methuen, p. xv.
6. Freeman, Mark. 2010. *Hindsight*. New York: Oxford University Press, p.178.
7. Ricoeur, Paul. 2004. *Memory, History, Forgetting*. Chicago: University of Chicago Press, p. 383.
8. Warnock, Mary. 2011. Personal interview (March 7).
9. Warnock, ' "Introduction" to Jean Paul Sartre,' xvii.
10. Nichols, Shaun, ed. 2006. *The Architecture of the Imagination: New Essays on Pretence, Possibility, and Fiction*. Oxford: Clarendon Press, p. 2.
11. Sartre, J. P. (19401972). *The Psychology of Imagination*. London: Methuen, p. 211.
12. Sartre, *The Psychology of Imagination*, 215.
13. Stoetzler, M. and N. Yuval-Davis (2002) "Standpoint Theory, Situated Knowledge—and the Situated Imagination." *Feminist Theory* 3(3):315–334.
14. Stoetzler and Yuval-Davis, "Standpoint Theory," 321.
15. Stoetzler and Yuval-Davis, "Standpoint Theory," 316.
16. Stoetzler and Yuval-Davis, "Standpoint Theory," 325.
17. Brockmeier, Jens. 2000. "Autobiograpjical Time." *Narrative Inquiry* 10(1): 53.
18. Orgad, Shani. 2012. *Media Representation and the Global Imagination*. Cambridge: Polity, p. xi.
19. Orgad, Shani, *Media Representation*, 43–47.
20. Warnock, Mary. 1994. *Imagination and Time*. Oxford, UK: Blackwell, p. 21.
21. Levinas, Emmanuel. 1972/2003. *Humanism of the Other*. Chicago: University of Illinois Press, p. xxvii.
22. Ascherson, Neal 2008. 'Introduction' in Kapuściński, Ryszard *The Other* London: Verso, p. 5.
23. Kapuściński, Ryszard. 2008. *The Other*. London: Verso, p. 19.
24. Kapuściński, *The Other*, 34.

25. Riessman, C. 2008. *Narrative Methods for the Human Sciences*. London: Sage, p. 139.
26. Kapuściński, *The Other*, 86.
27. A similar point is made, albeit more acerbically, by Bob Dylan in his song "Positively 4th Street:

> I wish that for just one time
> You could stand inside my shoes
> And just for that one moment
> I could be you
> Yes, I wish that for just one time
> You could stand inside my shoes
> You'd know what a drag it is
> To see you
> Dylan (1965)

28. Cocking, J. M., ed. 1991. *Imagination: A Study in the History of Ideas*. London: Routledge, p. vii.
29. Proud, Linda. 2012. "The Sweet Voice of Reason." In *The Gist: A Celebration of the Imagination*, edited by Lindsay Clarke, p. 127. UK: The Write Factor.
30. Stoetzler and Yuval-Davis, "Standpoint Theory," 316.
31. Brinkman, Svend 2012. *Qualitative Inquiry in Everyday Life*. London: Sage, p. 16.
32. Douglas, Jack (1970). *Understanding Everyday Life: Toward the reconstruction of sociological knowledge*. Rutgers, NJ: Aldine Publishing Company, p. 3.
33. Brinkman, *Qualitative Inquiry*.
34. Ferguson, H. 2009. *Self-Identity and Everyday Life*. Abingdon, UK: Routledge.
35. Highmore, Ben. 2010. *Ordinary Lives: Studies in the Everyday*. London: Routledge.
36. Pink, S. 2012. *Situating Everyday Life: Practices and Places*. London: Sage.
37. Scott, S. 2009. *Making Sense of Everyday Life*. Cambridge, UK: Polity.
38. Sherringham, M. 2009. *Everyday Life: Theories and Practices from Surrealism to the Present*. Oxford, UK: Oxford University Press.
39. Ferguson, *Self-Identity*, 160.
40. Geertz, C. 1973. *The Interpretation of Cultures: Selected Essays*. New York: Basic Books, p. 53.
41. Geertz, *The Interpretation of Cultures*, 44.
42. Bruner, Jerome. 1986. *Actual Minds Possible Worlds*. Cambridge: Harvard University Press, p. 26.

Chapter 2
1. Cashford, Jules. 2012. "Mythic Imagination." In *The Gist: A Celebration of the Imagination*, edited by Lindsay Clarke. UK: The Write Factor, p. 43.
2. Heidgger, Martin. 1994. *Basic Questions of Philosophy*, trans. R. Rojcewicz and A. Shuwer Bloomington: Indiana University Press, p. 143.
3. Lamont, Peter. 2004a. *The Rise of the Indian Rope Trick: The Biography of a Legend*. Boston: Little Brown, pp. 80–81.
4. Lamont, *The Rise of the Indian Rope Trick*, 77–84.
5. Lamont, *The Rise of the Indian Rope Trick*, xxii.
6. Lamont, *The Rise of the Indian Rope Trick*, 41–42.
7. Lamont, Peter. 2004b. The Rediff Interview (August 17–19). http://www.rediff.com/news/2004/aug/19inter.htm (Accessed May 1, 2009).
8. Lamont, The Rediff Interview.

9. Steinmeyer, J. 1998. *Art and Artifice and Other Essays on Illusion*. New York: Carroll and Graf, p. 80.
10. Steinmeyer, *Art and Artifice*, 79.
11. Steinmeyer, *Art and Artifice*, 78.
12. Steinmeyer, *Art and Artifice*, 78–79.
13. Steinmeyer, *Art and Artifice*, 84.
14. Gallagher, L. Spring 2006. "Casting the Spell: Magic in Book." *The LaTrobe Journal* 28: 85.
15. Palmer, J.-I. 2004. "Review of Jim Steinmeyer's Hiding the Elephant." http://www.nthposition.com/hidingtheelephant.php (Accessed May 1, 2009).
16. Gallagher, "Casting the Spell," 81.
17. To watch a video clip which Wiseman uncovered of these images, go to 'Early Magic Trick' on YouTube.
18. Lachapelle, S. 2008. "From the Stage to the Laboratory: Magicians, Psychologists, and the Science of Illusion." *Journal of the History of the Behavioural Sciences* 44(4): 319–334.
19. Lachapelle, "From the Stage to the Laboratory," 319–334.
20. Jha, A. 2005. "Bursting the Magic Bubble." *The Guardian* (July 28).
21. Jha, "Bursting the Magic Bubble."
22. Kuhn, G. 2009. Home page http://www.dur.ac.uk/gustav.kuhn/Media/Examples.htm (Accessed May 1, 2009).
23. Jha, "Bursting the Magic Bubble."
24. Kuhn, G., A. Amlani, and R. Rensink. 2008. "Towards a science of magic." *Trends in Cognitive Science* 12(9): 349–354.
25. Kuhn, Amlani, and Rensink, "Towards a science of magic," 350.
26. Wiseman, R. 2007. *Quirkology: The Curious Science of Everyday Lives*. London: Macmillan.
27. Lamont, The Rediff Interview.
28. Kuhn, Amlani, and Rensink, "Towards a science of magic," 350.
29. Hyman, R. 1989. "The Psychology of Deception." *Annual Review of Psychology* 40: 133–154.
30. Hyman, "The Psychology of Deception," 136.
31. Hyman, "The Psychology of Deception," 136–137.
32. Lamont, P., and R. Wiseman. 1999. *Magic in Theory: An Introduction to the Theoretical and Psychological Elements of Conjuring*. Hatfield, UK: University of Hertfordshire Press, p. 66.
33. Lamont and Wiseman, *Magic in Theory*, 66.
34. Burger, E., and Neale, R. 1994. *Magic and Meaning*. Seattle: Hermetic Press, pp. 1–4.
35. Lamont and Wiseman, *Magic in Theory*, 67.
36. Lamont and Wiseman, *Magic in Theory*, 57.
37. Steinmeyer, J. 1998. *Art and Artifice and Other Essays on Illusion*. New York: Carroll and Graf, p. 8.
38. BBC Radio 4. July 23, 2008. "Now you see it, now you don't." *Today Show*. http://news.bbc.co.uk/today/hi/today/newsid_7520000/7520043.stm (Accessed May 1, 2009).
39. Buchanan, R. July 29, 2005. "Watch My Hand Deceive You." BBC Online. http://news.bbc.co.uk/1/hi/sci/tech/4726547.stm (Accessed May 1, 2009).
40. Buchanan, "Watch My Hand."
41. Lamont, The Rediff Interview.

42. Hyman, R. 1989. "The Psychology of Deception." *Annual Review of Psychology* 40: 135–136.
43. Kawamoto, W. 2009. "Interview with Arthur Trace: The creative process." About. com: Magic and Illusion. http://magic.about.com/od/biosonfamousmagicians/a/arthurtraceqa.htm (Accessed May 1, 2009).
44. Steinmeyer, *Art and Artifice*, 7.
45. Apfelbaum, E. 2001. "The Dread: An Essay on Communication across Cultural Boundaries." *International Journal of Critical Psychology* (4): 31.
46. Fernandez, J. 1986. *Persuasions and Performances: The Play of Tropes in Culture.* Bloomington: Indiana University Press, p. 223.
47. Andrews, Molly. 2007. *Shaping History: Narratives of Political Change.* Cambridge, UK: Cambridge University Press, p. 47.
48. For a more elaborate discussion on the legacy of this article, see Atkinson, Paul, Amanda Coffey, and Sara Delamont. 2003. *Key Themes in Qualitative Research: Continuities and Changes.* Walnut Creek, CA: AltaMira Press, pp. 79–82, chapter 3: Whose Side Are We On: Inherent Tensions.
49. Becker, Howard. 1970. *Sociological Work: Method and Substance.* Chicago: Adline, p. 131.
50. Atkinson, Amanda, and Sara, *Key Themes in Qualitative Research*, 79–82.
51. Brockmeier, Jens. 2009. "Reaching for Meaning: Human Agency and the Narrative Imagination." *Theory and Psychology* 19(2): 230.
52. Ndlovu, Siyanda. 2008. *The Story of One Black Man: Graduate Guest Seminar Presentation.* University of KwaZulu-Natal, p. 8.
53. Ndlovu, *The Story of One Black Man*, 6.
54. Ndlovu, *The Story of One Black Man*, 7.
55. Ndlovu, *The Story of One Black Man*, 8.
56. Ndlovu, Siyanda. 2013. Portfolio of Doctoral Work Submitted to the University of KwaZulu-Natal November 2012. Degree awarded 2013, p. 76.
57. Reading Ndlovu's account of the reality and non-reality of 'race', I cannot help but remember the famous Thomas Theorem (1928:571–572) 'If men define situations as real, then they are *real in their consequences*'. To wish race way, Ndlovu argues, is to deny centuries of real, lived oppression.
58. Ndlovu, Siyanda. 2013. Portfolio of Doctoral Work Submitted to the University of KwaZulu-Natal November 2012. Degree awarded 2013, p. 13.
59. Lamont, The Rediff Interview.

Chapter 3

1. Furman, Frida Kerner. 1997. *Facing the Mirror: Older Women and Beauty Shop Culture.* New York: Routledge, p. 184.
2. De Beauvoir, Simone. 1970. *Old Age.* Middlesex, UK: Penguin, p. 12.
3. Bytheway, Bill. 2011. *Unmasking Age: The Significance of Age for Social Research.* Bristol: Policy Press, p. 21.
4. De Beauvoir, *Old Age*, 17.
5. Bytheway, *Unmasking Age*, 205.
6. Bytheway, *Unmasking Age*, 187.
7. Baars, Jan. 2010. "Philosophy of Aging, Time, and Finitude." In *A guide to Humanistic Studies in Aging: What Does It Mean to Grow Old?* edited by Thomas R.Cole, Ruth Ray, and Robert Kastenbaum. Baltimore, MD: The Johns Hopkins University Press, p. 108.
8. Kermode. 2007. "Not Just Yet." *London Review of Books* 29(24):17–18.

9. Gullette Margaret. 2008. "What Exactly Has Age Got to Do with It? My Life in Critical Age Studies." *Journal of Aging Studies* 2(22): 190.
10. On occasion, of course gerontologists have reflected on their own aging. One very successful example of this was the 2008 Special Issue of the *Journal of Aging Studies*, 'Coming of Age: Critical Gerontologists Reflect on Their Own Aging, Age Research and the Making of Critical Gerontology'—a collection of articles which is outstanding in its integration of personal experience with rigorous scholarship.
11. Moody, Harry R. 1992. "Gerontology and Critical Theory." *The Gerontologist* 3: 295.
12. Hendricks, Jon. 2008. "Coming of Age." *Journal of Aging Studies* 2(22): 113.
13. Holstein, Martha. 2006. "On Being an Aging Woman." In *Age Matters: Realigning Feminist Thinking*, edited by Calasanti, Toni M. and Kathleen F. Slevin. London: Routledge, p. 313.
14. Holstein, Martha. 2006. "On Being an Aging Woman," 327.
15. Holstein, Martha. 2006. "On Being an Aging Woman," 330.
16. Andrews, Molly. 2009. "The Narrative Complexity of Successful Aging." *International Journal of Sociology and Social Policy*, Special issue on Theorising Aging Studies 29/1-2: 76.
17. May, William. 1985. "The Virtues and Vices of the Elderly." In *What Does It Mean to Grow Old?* edited by Thomas Cole and Sally Gadow, 43–61. *Reflections from the Humanities*. Durham, NC: Duke University Press.
18. Andrews, "The Narrative Complexity of Successful Aging."
19. Holstein, Martha. 2006. "On Being an Aging Woman," 330.
20. Terkel, Studs. 1995. *Coming of Age: The Story of our Century by Those Who've Lived It*. New York: St. Martin's Griffin, p. xxvi.
21. Abadie, Michelle, and Mike Cast. 2010. *8000 Years of Wisdom: 100 Octogenarians Share Their Lessons Learned from Life*. Mid Glamorgan, Wales: Accent Press.
22. Alford, Henry. 2009. *How to Live: A Search for Wisdom from Old People (While they are still on this earth)* New York: Twelve.
23. BBC News. March 7, 2008. "Poem honours WW1 Veteran aged 109." http://news.bbc.co.uk/1/hi/england/somerset/7279861.stm (Accessed October 24, 2012).
24. *New York Times*.1997. "Jeanne Calment, World's Elder, Dies at 122." (August 5). http://www.nytimes.com/1997/08/05/world/jeanne-calment-world-s-elder-dies-at-122.html (Accessed October 24, 2010).
25. It has been rumoured that Kim Jong-il used to inject himself 'with blood from healthy young virgins in a bid to slow the ageing process' (Jha 2012). The research of Saul Villeda of Stanford University has scientifically explored the possibility of 'rejuvenat[ing] the brains of old animals by injecting them with blood from the young' (Jha 2012). The quest for the Holy Grail continues.
26. When people of different generations live under the same roof, they have the opportunity to witness first hand different stages of the life cycle, stimulating memories and imaginings of their own lives in the past and future. In a conversation with Mary Warnock, who was at the time 87 years old, she told me that for the previous six months she had 'been living in close proximity with an eight year old child' who she described as 'a dancer by nature, tremendously conscious of her own body, what it can do and what it can't do'—in other words, though they were separated in age by nearly eight decades, nonetheless they shared a consciousness about their physical capabilities.
27. Furman, *Facing the Mirror*, 2.

28. *New York Times*. 2010. "Robert Butler, Aging Expert, Is Dead at 83." (July 7) http://www.nytimes.com/2010/07/07/health/research/07butler.html (Accessed October 24, 2012).
29. Shankardass, Mala Kapur. 2010. "Aging with Dignity." *The Hindu* (August 7).
30. Beneviste, Pip. 2008. *The Pink House: An Autobiography* Tunisia: Avant Garde Editions, p. 8.
31. Wood, Michael. 2006. "Introduction." In *On Late Style: Music and Literature Against the Grain,* edited by Edward Said. London: Bloomsbury, p. xi.
32. Said, Edward. 2004. "Thoughts on Late Style." *London Review of Books* 26(15): 3–7.
33. Said, "Thoughts on Late Style."
34. Kureishi, Hanif. 2006. Amazon Product Description. *On Late Style: Music and Literature Against the Grain.*
35. Hill, Rosemary. 2010. "What We Are Last." *London Review of Books* 32(20): 25–26.
36. Sundaram, Chitra. 2007. "Love and Authenticity in the Age of Anxiety—Dance and Ageing." *Animated: The Community Dance Magazine*: 11. http://www.communitydance.org.uk/DB/animated-library/love-and-authenticity-in-the-age-of-anxiety-dance-.html?ed=14048 (Accessed September 2, 2013).
37. Wyatt-Brown, Anne. 2010. "Resilience and Creativity in Aging: The Realms of Silver." In *A Guide to Humanistic Studies in Aging: What Does It Mean to Grow Old?* edited by Thomas R. Cole, Ruth Ray, and Robert Kastenbaum. Baltimore, MD: The Johns Hopkins University Press, p. 57.
38. Hepworth, Mike. 2000. *Stories of Aging.* Milton Keynes, UK:Open University Press.
39. Hepworth, *Stories of Aging*, 4.
40. Wyatt-Brown, "Resilience and Creativity in Aging," 57.
41. Marquez, Gabriel Garcia. 1988. *Love in the Time of Cholera.* Harmondsworth, UK: Penguin, p. 50.
42. Bhatti, Mark. 2006. "'When I'm in the garden, I can create my own paradise': Homes and gardens in later life." *The Sociological Review* 54(2): 338.
43. Bhatti, "When I'm in the garden," 328.
44. Cicero, Marcus. 44 B.C./1951. "De Senectute." In *The Basic Works of Cicero.* New York: Modern Library, p. 146.
45. *The Guardian*. 2006. "The Oldie Issue." *Weekend* (October 28), p. 91.
46. *The Guardian*, "The Oldie Issue," 94.
47. See, for instance, the 1998 Mass Observation directive 'The Garden and Gardening', and the website 'Imagining the Garden' which provides materials from this directive http://www.rgs.org/NR/exeres/9F89AA39-ECF7-4C8B-9 8C5-0561ACC10262.htm).
48. Judt, Tony. 2010. "Night." *The New York Review of Books* (January 14).
49. Berman, Phillip and Connie Goldman, eds. 1992. *The Ageless Spirit* New York: Random House, p. 31.
50. Holstein, Martha. 2006. "On Being an Aging Woman," 326.
51. Holstein, Martha. 2006. "On Being an Aging Woman," 313.
52. Holstein, Martha. 2006. "On Being an Aging Woman," 313.
53. Daffern, Eileen. 2007. *Essays on a Life: Politics, Peace and the Personal.* Hove, UK: B & M Publishing, p. 224.
54. May, William. 1985. "The Virtues and Vices of the Elderly." In *What Does It Mean to Grow Old?* edited by Thomas Cole and Sally Gadow. *Reflections from the Humanities.* Durham, NC: Duke University Press.
55. Furman, *Facing the Mirror*, 95.

56. Daffern, *Essays on a Life*, 222.
57. Erikson, E.H. 1959. *Identity and The Life Cycle Selected Papers*. Madison. CT: International University Press, Inc., p. 98.
58. Butler, Robert. 1963. "The Life Review: An Interpretation of Reminiscence in the Aged." *Psychiatry* 26: 66.
59. Randall, W. L. 2013. "The Importance of Being Ironic. Narrative Openness and Personal Resilience in Later Life." *Gerontologist* 53(1): 9.
60. Randall, "The Importance of Being Ironic," 10.
61. Randall, "The Importance of Being Ironic," 12.
62. Freeman, Mark. 2010. *Hindsight*. New York: Oxford University Press, p. 4.
63. Randall, "The Importance of Being Ironic," 13.
64. Freud, Sigmund. 1915. "On Transience" Translation by James Strachey http://www.freuds-requiem.com/transience.html
65. Freud, "On Transience."
66. Daffern, *Essays on a Life*, 230.
67. Andrews, Molly. 1997. "Life review in the context of acute social transition: The case of East Germany." *British Journal of Social Psychology* 36: 273–290.
68. Daffern, *Essays on a Life*, 231.
69. Andrews, M. 2006. "Exploring cultural boundaries" in Clandinin, J., ed. *Handbook of narrative inquiry*. London: Sage.
70. Daffern, *Essays on a Life*, 225.
71. Katz, Stephen, and Kevin McHugh. 2010. "Age, Meaning and Place." In *A Guide to Humanistic Studies in Aging: What Does It Mean to Grow Old?* edited by Thomas R. Cole, Ruth Ray, and Robert Kastenbaum. Baltimore, MD: The Johns Hopkins University Press, p. 278–279.
72. Cicero, 44 B.C./1951. "De Senectute," 158.
73. Améry, Jean. 1994. *On Aging: Revolt and Resignation* Bloomington: Indiana University Press, p. 123.
74. Améry, *On Aging*, 108.
75. Améry, *On Aging*, 109.
76. Larkin, Philip. "The Old Fools." *The Complete Poems of Philip Larkin*.
77. Cicero, 44 B.C./1951. "De Senectute," 153.
78. Butler, Robert. Jul/Aug 2008. "Spearheading the Longevity Revolution: Patrick Perry Interviews Robert Butler." *Saturday Evening Post* 280(4): 56.
79. Kermode. 2007. "Not Just Yet." *London Review of Books* 29(24):17–18.
80. Nuland, Sherwin. 1993. *How We Die: Reflections of Life's Final Chapter*, new ed. Vintage Books, p. 261.
81. Nuland, *How We Die*, 267.
82. Améry, *On Aging*, 123–124.
83. Furman, *Facing the Mirror*, 158.
84. One of the most poignant pieces of writing on surviving one's children is by the poet Denise Riley: her son's

sudden death has dropped like a guillotine blade to slice right through my old expectation that my days would stream onwards into my coming life... What does your old philosophy of endurance mean, when there's no longer any temporality left in which to wait it out?... Your old stance is changed, not by melancholy, but by the shattering of that underlying intuition of moving in time, which you can't register until it's collapsed. If time was once flowing, extended, elongated—a river, a road, a ribbon—now the river is dammed, the road blocked, the ribbon slashed. Well-worn metaphors all shot to pieces... You share the 'timeless time' of the dead child. (Riley 2012)

We age, and experience our selves as passing through time, as part and parcel of the relationships which constitute our lives. When those relationships are severed, our sense of living in time—the heart of our narrative identity—is radically altered.

85. Nuland, *How We Die*, 267.
86. Moat, John. 2012a. "Unfinished Business." In *The Gist: A Celebration of the Imagination*, edited by Lindsay Clarke. UK: The Write Factor.

Chapter 4

1. hooks, bell. 1994. *Teaching to Transgress: Education as the Practice of Freedom* New York: Routledge, p. 207.
2. Warnock, Mary. 1976. *Imagination*. London: Faber and Faber, p. 202.
3. Warnock, Mary. 1989. *Universities: Knowing Our Minds*. London: Chatto & Windus, p. 37.
4. Warnock, *Imagination*, 207.
5. Moat, John. 2012b. "The Gist of Arvon." In *The Gist: A Celebration of the Imagination*, edited by Lindsay Clarke. UK: The Write Factor, p. 24.
6. Murphy, Peter "Discovery" in Murphy, Peter, Michael Peter, Simon Marginson. 2010. Imagination: *Three models of imagination in the age of the knowledge economy*. Oxford: Peter Lang, p. 103.
7. Warnock, *Imagination*, 196.
8. Warnock, *Imagination*, 206.
9. Warnock, *Imagination*, 206.
10. Murphy, "Discovery," 87.
11. John Moat offers the following characterization of the current state of the education system in the UK, where public funding for universities has been cut by 80%, while tuition fees have trebled:

    If it's true that generosity is a feature of the creative Imagination, it would seem obvious why the prevailing system of education should generally ignore it: the 'system' doesn't do business with generosity. In fact quite the opposite—it is openly extortionate. Teachers for the most are, or would be, generous—but not the system. If it gives, it gives only on condition that it will be repaid, and with interest (Moat 2012b, 27).

12. Murphy, "Discovery," 17.
13. Murphy, "Discovery," 89.
14. Almond, David. March 10, 2013. *BBC Radio 4*, Desert Island Discs.
15. Almond, *BBC Radio 4*.
16. Freire, Paulo. 2005. *Teachers as Cultural Workers: Letters to Those Who Dare to Teach* Boulder, CO: Westview Press, p. 31.
17. Freire, *Teachers as Cultural Workers*, 107.
18. Freire, *Teachers as Cultural Workers*, 6.
19. Campbell, Elizabeth. 2003. *The Ethical Teacher* Maidenhead: Open University Press, p. xii.
20. Palmer, Parker. 2003. "The Heart of a Teacher: Identity and Integrity in Teaching." In *The Jossey-Bass Reader on Teaching*. San Francisco: Jossey Bass, p. 5.
21. Goodson, Ivor F. 2005. *Learning, Curriculum and Life Politics*. London: Routledge, p. 24.
22. Freire, *Teachers as Cultural Workers*, 102.
23. Greene, May. 2003. "Teaching as Possibility: A Light in Dark Times." In *The Jossey-Bass Reader on Teaching*. San Francisco: Wiley, p. 62.

24. hooks, *Teaching to Transgress*, 21.
25. Pat Sikes describes how the experience of becoming a mother affected her teaching:

    Now that I had become a mother and was aware of how significant that experience was for my professional life, the process of 'othering' was interrupted...(Sikes 1997, 10)
       I share Sikes' experience of a shifting consciousness of myself both in and outside of the classroom which accompanied my becoming a parent; however, I am also aware that some students in my class might not be parents, and it is important not to exchange one dimension of 'othering' (being a parent) with another (having no children of one's own). In a similar vein, Wurtele (2011) writes: 'I am required to be present in the classroom as a cyclist, a concertgoer, a mother, a dogwalker—in other words a whole person—a citizen of my many intersecting communities' (p. 96). The challenge is to strike a balance of being willing to locate oneself without assuming that that particular situatedness applies to all.

26. Goodson, *Learning, Curriculum*, 14.
27. Ings, Welby. 2011. "An Assortment of Small Anomalies." in *Inspiring Academics: Learning with the World's Great University Teachers*, edited by Iain Hay. Milton Keynes, UK: Open University Press, p. 89.
28. Goodson, I. F. 1981. "Life History and the Study of Schooling." *Interchange*, 11(4): 69.
29. Clandinin, Jean, Janice Huber, Marilyn Huber, M. Shaun Murphy, Ann Murray Orr, Marni Peace, and Pam Steeves. 2006. *Composing Diverse Identities: Narrative Inquiries into the Interwoven Lives of Children and Teachers* London: Routledge.
30. Clandinin, D. J., and Connelly, F.M. 1998. "Stories to Live By: Narrative Understandings of School Reform." *Curriculum Inquiry* 28: 160–161.
31. Clandinin, Huber, Huber, Murphy, Orr, Peace, and Steeves, *Composing Diverse Identities*, 8.
32. Goodson, *Learning, Curriculum*, 229.
33. Goodson, *Learning, Curriculum*, 230.
34. Du Sautoy, Marcus. June 12, 2013. Interviewed by Libby Purves for BBC Radio 4's Programme "Midweek."
35. Andrews, Molly. 2010. "Learning from Stories, Stories of Learning." *Education Canada* Special Issue on Marginalized Youth 50(5): 29.
36. Moat, John. 2012a. "Unfinished Business." In *The Gist: A Celebration of the Imagination*, edited by Lindsay Clarke. UK: The Write Factor, p. 212.
37. Fried, Robert L. 2003. "Passionate Teaching." In *The Jossey-Bass Reader on Teaching*. San Francisco: Jossey-Bass and Wiley, p. 43.
38. Fried, "Passionate Teaching," 46.
39. Murphy, "Discovery," 108.
40. Murphy, "Discovery," 129.
41. Murphy, "Discovery," 108.
42. Loeffler, T.A. 2011. "I Teach as the Mountains Teach Me." In *Inspiring Academics: Learning with the World's Great University Teachers*, edited by Iain Hay. Milton Keynes, UK: Open University Press, p. 29.
43. Moat, "The Gist of Arvon," 27.
44. Edelstein, Wolfgang. 2011. "Education for Democracy: Reasons and Strategies." *European Journal of Education*. 46(1): 127.
45. Nussbaum, Martha. 2010a. *Not for Profit: Why Democracy Needs the Humanities*. Princeton: Princeton University Press, p. 2.

46. Nussbaum, *Not for Profit*, 25.
47. Nussbaum, *Not for Profit*, 25-26.
48. Kohlberg, Lawrence. 1981. *The Philosophy of Moral Development*. San Francisco: Harper & Row.
49. Kohlberg, Lawrence. 1984. *The Psychology of Moral Development*. San Francisco: Harper & Row.
50. Nussbaum, M. 1997. *Cultivating Humanity*. Cambridge, MA: Harvard University Press, pp. 10-11.
51. Harmon, James L., ed. 2002. *Take My Advice: Letters to the Next Generation from People Who Know a Thing or Two*. New York: Simon and Schuster, p. 177.
52. Nussbaum, *Cultivating Humanity*, 85.
53. Modell, Arnold. 2003. *Imagination and the Meaningful Brain*. Cambridge, MA: MIT Press, pp. 175-176.
54. Nussbaum, *Not for Profit*, 95.
55. Nussbaum, *Cultivating Humanity*, 91, 99.
56. von Wright, Moira. 2002. "Narrative Imagination and Taking the Perspective of Others." *Studies in Philosophy and Education* 21(4-5): 412.
57. Warnock, *Imagination*, 197.
58. von Wright, "Narrative Imagination," 414.
59. Nussbaum, Martha. 2010b. 'The fragility of goodness' http://www.pange-aprogress.com/1/post/2010/08/the-fragility-of-goodness-martha-nussbaum.html (Accessed December 11, 2012).
60. Nussbaum, Martha. 2002. "Education for Citizenship in an Era of Global Connection." *Studies in Philosophy and Education* 21: 300.
61. Nussbaum, "Education for Citizenship," 296.
62. hooks, *Teaching to Transgress*, 207.
63. Ings, "An Assortment of Small Anomalies," 94.

Chapter 5

1. Baker, Peter. 2013. "Inaugural Stresses Theme of Civil and Gay Rights—Saftey Net Praised." *The New York Times* (January 22, 2013) p. A1.
2. Scherer, Michael. 2012. "2012 Person of the Year: Barack Obama, the President." *Time* (December 19). http://poy.time.com/2012/12/19/person-of-the-year-barack-obama (Accessed April 1, 2013).
3. Stevenson, Richard. 2013. "A Call for Progressive Values: Evolved, Unapologetic and Urgent." *The New York Times* (January 22), A11.
4. Obama, Barack. 2013. Inaugural Address. *The Washington Post* (January 21).
5. Obama, Inaugural Address.
6. Some of the Obama books which have been recently published focus on his use of language. An example of this is Meider's (2009) *'Yes We Can': Barack Obama's Proverbial Rhetoric*, in which the author examines Obama's publications, and 229 public speeches, interviews and news conferences. Purveying these materials, Meider finds that Obama uses one proverb on average every 1.9 pages, and provides over 200 pages of examples of these.

   Gbotokuma's (2011) *Obamaenon: The Gospel of 'Glocal' Change, Hope, Understanding, and Leadership for Networking World* argues that 'Obama [and Barack, as he later indicates] as a word has enriched the English language' (2011:230). He provides a 70-page 'Barack Obama Glossary' in which he lists new phrases which he has found in the global print and electronic media, the Internet, and throughout the blogosphere. Examples of these include:

Barack Star—A term used for someone who is voting for Barack Obama and finds it cool to reference his name in normal speech

Barack-n-roll—The new tune of change

Obagasm—The overwhelming feeling of joy felt when one either hears Obama speak wisely on a delicate issue, or upon hearing about such sound judgments.

Not all entries reveal a positive evaluation of Obama. Each entry is followed by illustrative examples of where the term has been used.

7. McCrum, Robert. 2009. "When Obama Tells a Story, We Listen." *The Observer* (January 25).
8. Ryan, Paul (August 29 2012) Transcript: Rep Paul Ryan's Convention Speech. NPR News. http://www.npr.org/2012/08/29/160282031/transcript-rep-paul-ry ans-convention-speech (Accessed October 25, 2013).
9. Gonyea, Do. 2010. 'How's that hopey, changey stuff, Palin asks?' NPR Special Series: The Tea Party in America. http://www.npr.org/templates/story/story. php?storyId=123462728 (Accessed October 25, 2013).
10. Schama, Simon. 2009. "The Great Hope." *The Independent* (January 24). http:// www.independent.co.uk/news/presidents/simon-schama-the-great-hop e--barack-obama-1482927.html
11. Andrews, Molly. 2007. *Shaping History: Narratives of Political Change.* Cambridge, UK: Cambridge University Press.
12. Davis, Joseph, ed. 2002. *Stories of Change: Narrative and Social Movements.* Albany, NY: State University of New York Press.
13. Jackson, Michael. 2002. *The Politics of Storytelling: Violence, Transgression and Intersubjectivity.* Copenhagen: Museum Tusculanum Press.
14. Polletta, Francesca. 2006. *It Was Like a Fever: Storytelling in Protest and Politics.* Chicago: University of Chicago Press.
15. Selbin, Eric. 2011. *Revolution, Rebellion, Resistance: The Power of Story.* London: Zed Books.
16. Tilly, Charles. 2002. *Stories, Identities and Political Change.* New York: Rowman & Littlefield.
17. Zingaro, Linde. 2009. *Speaking Out: Storytelling for Social Change.* Walnut Creek, CA: Left Coast.
18. Selbin, *Revolution, Rebellion*, 30.
19. In this chapter, I focus on the written and spoken forms of political narratives, However, the importance of visual political narratives cannot be overstated. Obama's 2008 campaign offers a case in point, demonstrating the power of art to communicate the voice of a movement, epitomized by the now famous 'Hope' poster. As Miller writes

...the Obama campaign was challenged to communicate an alternative vision of what was possible... [the campaign] created space for artists to communicate Obama's message in ways that reflected their own artistic styles, personal histories, and communities. The result was a collection of art fueled by the personal passions and visions of the artist, but connected by a singular overall goal of changing this country... The images mattered. They connected to everyday voters in ways that traditional campaign literature couldn't (Miller 2009, 23–24).

20. Marqusee, Mike. 2012. "Let's Talk Utopia." In *Utopia*, edited by Ross Bradshaw. London: Five Leaves Publications, p. 10.
21. Andrews, *Shaping History*, 8.
22. Arendt, Hannah. 1958. *The Human Condition*. Chicago: University of Chicago Press, p. 50.
23. Arendt, *The Human Condition*, 50–51.
24. Zingaro, *Speaking Out*, 11.
25. Zingaro, *Speaking Out*, 11.
26. Field, S. 2006. "Beyond 'Healing': Trauma, Oral History and Regeneration." *Oral History* 34(1): 32.
27. Arendt, *The Human Condition*, 50.
28. Dienstag, J. F. 1997. *"Dancing in Chains": Narrative and Memory in Political Theory*. Stanford, CA: Stanford University Press, p. 206.
29. Obama's personal story might be unique in its particulars, but it is also a story which, at least in its broadest brush strokes—the son of a goat-herder ending up in the White House—resonates with the 19th century myth of Horatio Alger.
30. Obama, Barack. 2004. "2004 Democratic National Convention Keynote Address." (July 27). http://www.americanrhetoric.com/speeches/convention2004/barack-obama2004dnc (Accessed March 8, 2009).
31. Obama, Barack. 2006. Emily's List Annual Lunch, Washington, DC (May 11). http://www.guardian.co.uk/world/2009/jan/20/barack-obama-inauguration-speeches-1
32. Schama, "The Great Hope."
33. Cobb, William Jelani. 2010. *The Substance of Hope: Barack Obama and the Paradox of Progress*. New York: Walker, p. 20.
34. Amongst the many books which have appeared about Obama, there have been substantial biographies. Remnick's *The Bridge: The Life and Rise of Barack Obama* and Maraniss's *Barack Obama: The Story* are perhaps best known amongst these; together they amass nearly 1300 pages of information about Obama's life and family, stretching across four continents and four generations. Still, in terms of what the facts of his life mean—as opposed to the task of establishing those facts—there is no better guide than Obama himself.
35. That month, *Dreams of My Father* had been on the *New York Times* list for 122 weeks, and *Audacity to Hope* for 47 weeks (Wallace 2008).
36. Wallace, Milverton. 2008. "Brits Seems [sic] to Love (and Read Books of) the next U.S. President." http://www.brooklynron.com/dreams-from-my-father/
37. Even Toot's story was not 'just her story' as told by Obama. She was, he told a crowd when he annouced her passing, 'one of those quiet heroes we have all across America... who, they're not famous, their names aren't in the newspapers, but each and every day they work hard, look after their families, they sacrifice for their children and grandchildren... all they try to do is do the right thing.' (Zeleny 2008).
38. Still, it is unusual, even for public figures, to have written two autobiographies by their 45th birthday. 'The Obama story' was a critical tool which Obama employed to great effect during his formidable presidential campaign.
39. Ulaby, Neda. 2008. "Toni Morrison on Bondage and a Post-Racial Age." *Tell Me More*. NPR (December 10). http://www.npr.org/templates/story/story.php?storyId=98072491
40. Cobb, *The Substance of Hope*, 3.
41. Arendt, *The Human Condition*, 50.

42. Easton, Jaclyn, ed. 2009. *Inspire a Nation: Barack Obama's Most Electrifying Speeches from Day One of His Campaign through his Inauguration*. Publishing 180, p. 61.

43. I borrow this phrase from William Cobb (2010), 148.

44. Obama, Barack. 2005. "What I See in Lincoln's Eyes." *Time* (June 26). http://www.time.com

45. Easton, *Inspire a Nation*, 189.

46. Travers, K. 2009 "Obama Celebrates Lincoln's Bicentennial with 'Special Gratitude'." *Political Punch* (February 12). http://blogs.abcnews.com/political-punch/2009/02/obama-celebrate.html

47. When Obama was sworn into his second term as president on Martin Luther King Jr. Day, he used the Bible of the King family.

48. Obama, "What I See."

49. Amongst a number of characteristics which Obama and Lincoln might be seen to share, one of the most striking is their love of stories. Lincoln, by all accounts, was a great storyteller, and a great orator. On his style of delivery, he once commented: 'I am compelled by nature to speak slowly. I commence way back like the boys do when they want to get a good start. My weight and speed get momentum to jump far' (Blasidell 2005, 68), a description which could also apply to Obama. In 1901, there was a collection of stories attributed to Lincoln published under the title *Abe Lincoln Yarns and Stories* (Schwartz 1990, 99).

50. Obama, "What I See."

51. Polletta, Francesca. 2006. *It Was Like a Fever: Storytelling in Protest and Politics*. Chicago: University of Chicago Press, p. 19.

52. Polletta, *It Was Like a Fever*, 30.

53. Schwartz, Barry. 2000. *Abraham Lincoln and the Forge of National Memory*. Chicago: University of Chicago Press, p. 312.

54. Schwartz, *Abraham Lincoln*, 264.

55. Schwartz, Barry. 1990. "The Reconstruction of Abraham Lincoln." In *Collective Remembering*, edited by David Middleton and Derek Edwards. London: Sage, pp. 101–102.

56. Obama, Barack. 2009. "What the People Need Done." Abraham Lincoln Bicentennial (February 12). http://www.scribd.com/doc/12415216/Obama-Speech-at-Lincoln-Association-Banquet-Springfi eld-IL-21209Obama

57. Obama, "What the People Need Done."

58. Schwartz, "The Reconstruction," 83.

59. Gopnik, Adam. 2007. "Angels and Ages: Lincoln's Language and Its Legacy." *The New Yorker* (May 28) http://www.newyorker.com/reporting/2007/05/28/070528fa_fact_gopnik

60. Thomson, David. 2012. "Spielberg's *Lincoln* Is a Film for Our Political Moment." *The New Yorker* (November 13). http://www.tnr.com/article/books-and-arts/110113/spielbergs-lincoln-film-our-political-moment#

61. Stengel, Richard, Michael Scherer, and Radhika Jones. 2012. "Setting the Stage for a Second Term." *Time* (December 19). http://poy.time.com/2012/12/19/setting-the-stage-for-a-second-term/ (Accessed April 1, 2013).

62. Gopnik, Adam. 2012b. "Lincoln, Uncompromised." *The New Yorker* (November 24).

63. McCrum, Robert. 2009. "When Obama Tells a Story, We Listen." *The Observer* (January 25).

64. Easton, *Inspire a Nation*, 57.

65. Obama, Inaugural Address.

66. Obama, "2004 Democratic National Convention Keynote Address."

67. Although it is not unusual for politicians to hark back to the 'founding principles of our country', it is noteworthy when this invocation is made by one who embodies so many different traditions which were not originally intended for such inclusion.

68. Obama, "2004 Democratic National Convention Keynote Address."

69. This rhetoric of a unified American was again adopted by Obama in his acceptance speech on the night of the 2012 election.

70. AU News. Dec 2008. "African-Americans, Anger, Fear and Youth Propel Turnout to Highest Level Since 1964" [sic—the actual report says since 1960]. http://timeswampland.files.wordpress.com/2008/12/2008turnout-report_final11.pdf

71. Project Vote. 2008. "Minority Voting Surged in 2008 Election, According to Project Vote analysis." (November 25). http://projectvote.org/indexhttp://projectvote.org/index.php?id=80&tx_ttnews%5Btt_news%5D=2726&tx_ttnews%5BbackPid%5D=75&cHash=1fc560e9c7

72. Easton, *Inspire a Nation*, 145.

73. Cobb, *The Substance of Hope*, 2.

74. This was felt by some not only in the domestic sphere, but also internationally, epitomized by the placards which he encountered on his visit to South Africa in the summer of 2013 which read 'You've Changed'. Few of his supporters, at home or abroad, would have predicted the Obama administration policy on drones and national surveillance.

75. Rich, Frank. 2010. "Why Has He Fallen Short?" *New York Review of Books* (August 19).

76. Fallows, James. 2012.'Obama, Explained' *Atlantic Magazine* (March).

77. Davidson, Amy. 2012a. "The Malia Generation." *The New Yorker*. (November 7).

78. Rutenberg, Jim. 2012. "Raising G.O.P., Ryan Faults 'Missing' Leadership." *The New York Times* (August 29).

79. Davidson, "The Malia Generation."

80. Kurtz, Howard. 2012. "Democratic Convention Dilemma: Obama 2012 vs. Obama 2008." *The Daily Beast* (September 4).

81. Hardman, Isabel. 2012. "Obama Keeps that Hopey-Changey Thing Going in Victory Speech." *The Spectator* (November 7).

82. Davidson, "The Malia Generation."

83. Addressing the National Union of South African Students in Cape Town in 1966, Robert Kennedy told the crowd: 'Each time a man stands up for an ideal, or acts to improve the lot of others, or strikes out against injustice, he sends forth a tiny ripple of hope, and crossing each other from a million different centers of energy and daring, those ripples build a current which can sweep down the mightiest walls of oppression and resistance' (cited in Davidson 2012b).

84. Davidson, Amy. 2012b. "Obama's Tears and Ripples of Hope." *The New Yorker*. (November 9).

85. Kloppenberg, James T. 2011. *Reading Obama: Dreams, Hope, and the American Political Tradition*. Princeton, NJ: Princeton University Press, p. 263.

86. That time and narrative are intricately bound to one another is well established. What is striking about political narratives in general, and Obama's use of them in particular, is the importance of the relationship between narrative and timing. Critical historical moments are marked by the new and different kinds of stories which demand to be heard.

87. Carr, E. H. 1961. *What Is History?* Middlesex, UK: Penguin Books, p. 55.

88. Obama, "What the People Need Done."

89. Easton, *Inspire a Nation*, 194.

90. Schama, "The Great Hope."

91. Easton, *Inspire a Nation*, 199.

92. Obama's phrasing mirrored very closely this famous passage, thus again locating his own narrative within a broader history.

    We've got some difficult days ahead. But it doesn't matter with me now. Because I've been to the mountaintop...And I've looked over. And I've seen the promised land. I may not get there with you. But I want you to know tonight, that we, as a people, will get to the promised land. And I'm happy, tonight. I'm not worried about anything. I'm not fearing any man. Mine eyes have seen the glory of the coming of the Lord (King 1968).

93. Easton, *Inspire a Nation*, 148.
94. Easton, *Inspire a Nation*, 193.
95. Easton, *Inspire a Nation*, 200.
96. Easton, *Inspire a Nation*, 193.
97. These words echo Lincoln's well-known phrase, 'the better angels of our nature'.
98. Raban, Jonathan. 2009. "The Golden Trumpet." *The Guardian* (January 24). http://www.guardian.co.uk/world/2009/jan/24/barack-obama-inauguration-speech-presidency-president-review-jonathan-raban
99. Three years after the Supreme Court ruling of *Brown v. the Board of Education* (1954) outlawing the segregation of schools, nine African-American students registered for, and were blocked entry to, the all-white Little Rock Central High in Little Rock, Arkansas. They endured being spat upon and threatened with lynching as they tried to enter the school. Eventually the Federal government had to intervene. The Tuskegee Airmen were the country's first black military pilots and ground crew, who trained at Kuskegee Army Air Field in Alabama during the World War II. They included 900 black fighter and bomber pilots, more than 400 of whom served overseas.
100. Holland, Jesse. 2009. "Most of Little Rock Nine Headed to Inauguration." *The Seattle Times* (January 19). http://seattletimes.nwsource.com/html
101. Walters, Joanna. 2008. "'Little Rock Nine' prepare to celebrate day of victory." *The Observer* (December 28). http://www.guardian.co.uk/world/2008/dec
102. CNN News. January 22, 2009. "'Queen of Soul' not pleased with performance at inauguration." cnn.com.us http://edition.cnn.com/2009/US/01/22/lkl.aretha.franklin/index.html
103. "Remarks by the First Lady and the President at Final Campaign Rally—Des Moines, IA." November 6, 2012. http://www.whitehouse.gov/the-press-office/2012/11/06/remarks-first-lady-and-president-final-campaign-rally-des-moines-ia.
104. "Remarks by the First Lady and the President at Final Campaign Rally—Des Moines, IA."
105. At the luncheon following Obama's first inauguration, John Lewis asked Obama to autograph a sheet of paper, to mark the occasion. 'The 44th President of the United States wrote, "Because of you, John. Barack Obama"' (Remnick 2010, 579) acknowledging again the importance of the long political struggle that made his presidency possible.
106. Cobb, *The Substance of Hope*, 99.

Conclusion

1. Brockmeier, Jens. 2009. "Reaching for Meaning: Human Agency and the Narrative Imagination." *Theory and Psychology* 19(2): 213–233.
2. Brockmeier, "Reaching for Meaning," 227.
3. Cashford, Jules. 2012. "Mythic Imagination." In *The Gist: A Celebration of the Imagination*, edited by Lindsay Clarke. UK: The Write Factor, p. 44.

4. BBC News. March 7, 2008. "Poem honours WW1 Veteran aged 109." http://news.bbc.co.uk/1/hi/england/somerset/7279861.stm (Accessed October 24, 2012).
5. De Beauvoir, Simone. 1970. *Old Age*. Middlesex, UK: Penguin, p. 8.
6. Solnit, Rebecca. 2005. *A Field Guide to Getting Lost*. New York: Viking, p. 80.
7. Brockmeier, "Reaching for Meaning," 228.
8. De Beauvoir, *Old Age*, 10.
9. Andrews, Molly. 1991/re-issued 2008. *Lifetimes of Commitment: Aging, Politics, Psychology*. Cambridge: Cambridge University Press.
10. Warnock, Mary. 1940/1972. "Introduction" to Jean Paul Sartre *The Psychology of Imagination*. London: Methuen, p. 197.
11. Warnock, Mary. 1989. *Universities: Knowing Our Minds*. London: Chatto & Windus, p. 37.
12. D'Souza, Dinesh. 2010. "How Obama Thinks." *Forbes Magazine*. (September 27).
13. Solnit, *A Field Guide*, 10.
14. Solnit, *A Field Guide*, 14, 22, 24.
15. Brockmeier, "Reaching for Meaning," 215.
16. Brockmeier, "Reaching for Meaning," 217.
17. Brockmeier, "Reaching for Meaning," 227.
18. Hughes, Ted. 2012. "Myth and Education." In *The Gist: A Celebration of the Imagination* Clarke, edited by Lindsay. UK: The Write Factor, p. 7.
19. Sail, Lawrence. 2012. "Sixteens." *The Gist: A Celebration of the Imagination*, edited by L. Clarke. UK: The Write Factor, p. 92.
20. Brockmeier, Jens. 2004. "Possible Lives" In *Considering Counter-narratives: Narrating, resisting, making sense*, edited by Michael Bamberg and Molly Andrews. Amsterdam: John Benjamins.
21. Williams, Raymond. 1988. *Resources of Hope: Culture, Democracy, Socialism*. London: Verso.

BIBLIOGRAPHY

Abadie, Michelle and Mike Cast. 2010. *8000 Years of Wisdom: 100 Octogenarians Share Their Lessons Learned from Life*. Mid Glamorgan, Wales: Accent Press.

Adorno, Theodor W. (1938/2002) Spatstil Beethovens [Late Style in Beethoven], reprinted in *Essays on Music*, ed Richard Leppert. London: University of California Press.

Alford, Henry. 2009. *How to Live: A Search for Wisdom from Old People (While they are still on this earth)* New York: Twelve.

Almond, David. March 10, 2013. *BBC Radio 4*, Desert Island Discs.

Améry, Jean. 1994. *On Aging: Revolt and Resignation* Bloomington: Indiana University Press.

Andrews, Molly. 1991/re-issued 2008. *Lifetimes of Commitment: Aging, Politics, Psychology*. Cambridge: Cambridge University Press.

Andrews, Molly. 1997. "Life Review in the Context of Acute Social Transition: The Case of East Germany." *British Journal of Social Psychology* 36: 273–290.

Andrews, Molly. 2006. "Exploring cultural boundaries." *Handbook of Narrative Inquiry*, edited by J. Clandinin. London: Sage.

Andrews, Molly. 2007. *Shaping History: Narratives of Political Change*. Cambridge, UK: Cambridge University Press.

Andrews, Molly. 2009. "The Narrative Complexity of Successful Aging." *International Journal of Sociology and Social Policy*, Special issue on Theorising Aging Studies 29/1-2: 73–83.

Andrews, Molly. 2010. "Learning from Stories, Stories of Learning." *Education Canada* Special Issue on Marginalized Youth 50(5): 27–30.

Apfelbaum, E. 2001. "The Dread: An Essay on Communication across Cultural Boundaries." *International Journal of Critical Psychology* (4): 19–35.

Arendt, Hannah. 1958. *The Human Condition*. Chicago: University of Chicago Press.

Ascherson, Neal 2008. 'Introduction' in Kapuściński, Ryszard *The Other* London: Verso.

Atkinson, Paul, Amanda Coffey, and Sara Delamont. 2003. *Key Themes in Qualitative Research: Continuities and Changes*. Walnut Creek, CA: AltaMira Press.

AU News. Dec 2008. "African-Americans, Anger, Fear and Youth Propel Turnout to Highest Level Since 1964" [sic—the actual report says since 1960]. http://timeswampland.files.wordpress.com/2008/12/2008turnout-report_final11.pdf

Baars, Jan. 2010. "Philosophy of Aging, Time, and Finitude." In *A guide to Humanistic Studies in Aging: What Does It Mean to Grow Old?* edited by Thomas R. Cole, Ruth Ray, and Robert Kastenbaum. Baltimore, MD: The Johns Hopkins University Press.

Bain, Ken. 2004. *What the Best College Teachers Do*. Cambridge: Harvard University Press

Baker, Peter. 2013. "Inaugural Stresses Theme of Civil and Gay Rights—Saftey Net Praised." *The New York Times* (January 22, 2013) p. A1.

Ball, Stephen J., ed. 2004. *The RoutledgeFalmer Reader in Sociology of Education*. London: RoutledgeFalmer.

BBC News. March 7, 2008. "Poem honours WW1 Veteran aged 109." http://news.bbc.co.uk/1/hi/england/somerset/7279861.stm (Accessed October 24, 2012).

BBC Radio 4. July 23, 2008. "Now you see it, now you don't." *Today Show*. http://news.bbc.co.uk/today/hi/today/newsid_7520000/7520043.stm (Accessed May 1, 2009).

Becker, Howard. 1970. *Sociological Work: Method and Substance*. Chicago: Adline.

Beneviste, Pip. 2008. *The Pink House: An Autobiography* Tunisia: Avant Garde Editions.

Berman, Phillip and Connie Goldman, eds. 1992. *The Ageless Spirit* New York: Random House.

Bhatti, Mark. 2006. "'When I'm in the garden, I can create my own paradise': Homes and gardens in later life." *The Sociological Review* 54(2): 318–341.

Blaisdell, Bob, ed. 2005. *The Wit and Wisdom of Abraham Lincoln*. Mineola, NY: Dover.

Bradshaw, Ross, ed. 2012. *Utopia*. London: Five Leaves Publications.

Brinkman, Svend. 2012. *Qualitative Inquiry in Everyday Life*. London: Sage.

Brockmeier, Jens. 2000. "Autobiograpjical Time." *Narrative Inquiry* 10(1): 51–73.

Brockmeier, Jens. 2004. "Possible Lives in Bamberg," In *Considering Counter-narratives: Narrating, resisting, making sense*, edited by Michael Bamberg and Molly Andrews. Amsterdam: John Benjamins.

Brockmeier, Jens. 2009. "Reaching for Meaning: Human Agency and the Narrative Imagination." *Theory and Psychology* 19(2): 213–233.

Bruner, Jerome. 1986. *Actual Minds Possible Worlds* Cambridge: Harvard University Press.

Brunskill, Ian, ed. 2005. *Great Lives: A Century in Obituaries* London: Times Books.

Buchanan, R. July 29, 2005. "Watch My Hand Deceive You." BBC Online. http://news.bbc.co.uk/1/hi/sci/tech/4726547.stm (Accessed May 1, 2009).

Burger, E., and Neale, R. 1994. *Magic and Meaning*. Seattle: Hermetic Press.

Butler, Robert. 1963. "The Life Review: An Interpretation of Reminiscence in the Aged." *Psychiatry* 26: 65–70.

Butler, Robert. 1975. *Why Survive? Being Old in America*. New York: Harper & Row.

Butler, Robert. Jul/Aug 2008. "Spearheading the Longevity Revolution: Patrick Perry Interviews Robert Butler." *Saturday Evening Post* 280(4): 56.

Byteway Bill. 2011. *Unmasking Age: The Significance of Age for Social Research*. Bristol: Policy Press.

Calasanti, Toni M., and Kathleen F. Slevin, eds. 2006. *Age Matters: Realigning Feminist Thinking*. London: Routledge.

Cammarota, Julio, and Michelle Fine, eds. 2008. *Revolutionizing Education: Youth Participatory Action Research in Motion*. London: Routledge.

Campbell, Elizabeth. 2003. *The Ethical Teacher* Maidenhead: Open University Press.

Carr, E. H. 1961. *What Is History?* Middlesex, UK: Penguin Books.

Carter, Kathy. 1993. "The Place of Story in the Study of Teaching and Teacher Education." *Educational Researcher* 22(1): 5–12, 18.

Cashford, Jules. 2012. "Mythic Imagination." In *The Gist: A Celebration of the Imagination, edited by* Lindsay Clarke. UK: The Write Factor.

Cicero, Marcus. 44 B.C./1951. "De Senectute." In *The Basic Works of Cicero*. New York: Modern Library.

Clandinin, D. J., and Connelly, F.M.. 1998. "Stories to Live By: Narrative Understandings of School Reform." *Curriculum Inquiry* 28: 149–164.

Clandinin, Jean, Janice Huber, Marilyn Huber, M. Shaun Murphy, Ann Murray Orr, Marni Peace, and Pam Steeves. 2006. *Composing Diverse Identities: Narrative Inquiries into the Interwoven Lives of Children and Teachers* London: Routledge.

Clarke, Lindsay, ed. 2012. *The Gist: A Celebration of the Imagination*. UK: The Write Factor.

CNN News. January 22, 2009. "'Queen of Soul' not pleased with performance at inauguration." cnn.com.us http://edition.cnn.com/2009/US/01/22/lkl.aretha.franklin/index.html

Cobb, William Jelani. 2010. *The Substance of Hope: Barack Obama and the Paradox of Progress*. New York: Walker.

Cocking, J. M., ed. 1991. *Imagination: A Study in the History of Ideas*. London: Routledge.

Cohen, Richard A. 2003. "Introduction." In Emmanuel Levinas, *Humanism of the Other*. Chicago: University of Illinois Press.

Cole, Thomas R., Ruth Ray, and Robert Kastenbaum, eds. 2010. *A Guide to Humanistic Studies in Aging: What Does It Mean to Grow Old?* Baltimore, MD: The Johns Hopkins University Press.

Connelly, F. M., and D. J. Clandinin. 1999. *Shaping a Professional Identity: Stories of Educational Practice*. New York: Teachers College Press

Daffern, Eileen. 2007. *Essays on a Life: Politics, Peace and the Personal*. Hove, UK: B & M Publishing.

Dahlstrom, Jane, and Gerlese Åkerlind. 2011. "The What, Why and How of Inspiring Learning." In *Inspiring Academics: Learning with the World's Great University Teachers*, edited by Iaian Hay. Milton Keynes, UK: Open University Press.

The Daily Show with Jon Stewart (Nov 6 2012).

Davidson, Amy. 2012a. "The Malia Generation." *The New Yorker*. (November 7).

Davidson, Amy. 2012b. "Obama's Tears and Ripples of Hope." *The New Yorker*. (November 9).

Davis, Joseph, ed. 2002. *Stories of Change: Narrative and Social Movements*. Albany, NY: State University of New York Press.

De Beauvoir, Simone. 1970. *Old Age*. Middlesex, UK: Penguin.

de Certeau, Michele. 1984. *The Practice of Everyday Life*. Berkeley, CA: University of California Press.

Dienstag, J. F. 1997. *"Dancing in Chains": Narrative and Memory in Political Theory*. Stanford, CA: Stanford University Press.

Douglas, Jack. 1970. *Understanding Everyday Life: Toward the reconstruction of sociological knowledge*. Rutgers, NJ: Aldine Publishing Company.

D'Souza, Dinesh. 2010. "How Obama Thinks." *Forbes Magazine*. (September 27).

Du Sautoy, Marcus. June 12, 2013. Interviewed by Libby Purves for BBC Radio 4's Programme "Midweek."

Dylan, Bob. 1965. 'Positively 4th Street'. http://www.bobdylan.com/us/songs/positively-4th-street, retrieved 25 October 2013.

Easton, Jaclyn, ed. 2009. *Inspire a Nation: Barack Obama's Most Electrifying Speeches from Day One of His Campaign through his Inauguration*. Publishing 180.

Edelstein, Wolfgang. 2011. "Education for Democracy: Reasons and Strategies." *European Journal of Education*. 46(1): 127–137.

Emerson, Lisa. 2011. "I Am a Writer": Unlocking Fear and Releasing Possibility in the Classroom." In *Inspiring Academics: Learning with the World's Great University Teachers*, edited by Iain Hay. Milton Keynes, UK: Open University Press.

Erikson, E.H. 1959. Identity and The Life Cycle Selected Papers. Madison, CT: International University Press, Inc.

Erikson, Erik. 1963. *Childhood and Society* Harmondsworth, UK: Penguin.

Fairey, Shepard and Jennifer Gross, eds. 2009. *Art for Obama: Designing Manifest Hope and the Campaign for Change* New York: Abrams.

Fallows, James. 2012. 'Obama, Explained' *Atlantic Magazine* (March).

Ferguson, H. 2009. *Self-Identity and Everyday Life*. Abingdon, UK: Routledge.

Fernandez, J. 1986. *Persuasions and Performances: The Play of Tropes in Culture*. Bloomington: Indiana University Press.

Field, S. 2006. "Beyond 'Healing': Trauma, Oral History and Regeneration." *Oral History* 34(1): 31–42.

Free, Rhone. 2011. "On Scholarly Teaching—A Personal Account." In *Inspiring Academics: Learning with the World's Great University Teachers*, edited by Iain Hay. Milton Keynes, UK: Open University Press.

Freeman, Mark. 2010. *Hindsight*. New York: Oxford University Press.

Freire, Paulo. 2005. *Teachers as Cultural Workers: Letters to Those Who Dare to Teach* Boulder, CO: Westview Press.

Freud, Sigmund. 1901. *The Psychopathology of Everyday Life*. London: T. Fisher Unwin.

Freud, Sigmund. 1915. "On Transience" Translation by James Strachey. http://www.freuds-requiem.com/transience.html

Fried, Robert L. 2003. "Passionate Teaching." In *The Jossey-Bass Reader on Teaching*. San Francisco: Jossey-Bass and Wiley.

Furman, Frida Kerner. 1997. *Facing the Mirror: Older Women and Beauty Shop Culture*. New York: Routledge.

Gallagher, L. Spring 2006. "Casting the Spell: Magic in Book." *The LaTrobe Journal* 28: 71–85.

Gbotokuma, Zekeh S. 2011. *Obamaenon: The Gospel of 'Glocal' Change,Hope, Understanding, and Leadership for Networking World*. Champaign, IL: Common Ground.

Geertz, C. 1973. *The Interpretation of Cultures: Selected Essays* New York: Basic Books.

Goffman, E. 1959. *The Presentation of Self in Everyday Life*. New York: Anchor Books.

Gonyea, Do. 2010. 'How's that hopey, changey stuff, Palin asks?' NPR Special Series: The Tea Party in America. http://www.npr.org/templates/story/story.php?storyId=123462728 (Accessed October 25, 2013).

Goodson, Ivor F. 1981. "Life History and the Study of Schooling." *Interchange*, 11(4): 62–79.

Goodson, Ivor F. 2005. *Learning, Curriculum and Life Politics*. London: Routledge.

Goodson, Ivor and Pat Sikes. 2001. *Life History Research in Educational Settings: Learning from Lives*. Buckingham, UK: Open University Press.

Gopnik, Adam. 2007. "Angels and Ages: Lincoln's Language and Its Legacy." *The New Yorker* (May 28) http://www.newyorker.com/reporting/2007/05/28/070528fa_fact_gopnik

Gopnik, Adam. 2009. *Angels and Ages*. New York: Knopf.

Gopnik, Adam. 2012a. "Obama's Political Intelligence." *The New Yorker* (November 8).

Gopnik, Adam. 2012b. "Lincoln, Uncompromised." *The New Yorker* (November 24).

Greenberg, David. 2011. "Hope, Change, Nietzsche." *The New Republic* (May 26). http://www.presidency.ucsb.edu/ws/index.php?pid=102613

Greene, May. 2003. "Teaching as Possibility: A Light in Dark Times." In *The Jossey-Bass Reader on Teaching*. San Francisco: Wiley.

The Guardian. 2006. "The Oldie Issue." *Weekend* (October 28).

Gullette Margaret. 2008. "What Exactly Has Age Got to Do with It? My Life in Critical Age Studies." *Journal of Aging Studies* 2(22): 189–195.

Hardman, Isabel. 2012. "Obama Keeps that Hopey-Changey Thing Going in Victory Speech." *The Spectator* (November 7).

Harmon, James L., ed. 2002. *Take My Advice: Letters to the Next Generation from People Who Know a Thing or Two*. New York: Simon and Schuster.

Harris, P. 1996. *The Art of Astonishment: Pieces of Strange to Unleash the Moment*. A-1 Multimedia.

Hay, Iain. 2011. *Inspiring Academics: Learning with the World's Great University Teachers*. Milton Keynes, UK: Open University Press.

Heidgger, Martin. 1994. *Basic Questions of Philosophy*, trans. R. Rojcewicz and A. Shuwer Bloomington: Indiana University Press.

Hendricks, Jon. 2008. "Coming of Age." *Journal of Aging Studies* 2(22): 109–114.

Hepworth, Mike. 2000. *Stories of Aging*. Milton Keynes, UK:Open University Press.

Highmore, Ben. 2010. *Ordinary Lives: Studies in the Everyday*. London: Routledge.

Hill, Rosemary. 2010. "What We Are Last." *London Review of Books* 32(20): 25–26.

Holland, Jesse. 2009. "Most of Little Rock Nine Headed to Inauguration." *The Seattle Times* (January 19). http://seattletimes.nwsource.com/html

Holstein, Martha. 2006. "On Being an Aging Woman." In *Age Matters: Realigning Feminist Thinking*, edited by Calasanti, Toni M. and Kathleen F. Slevin. London: Routledge.

hooks, bell. 1994. *Teaching to Transgress: Education as the Practice of Freedom* New York: Routledge.

Hughes, Ted. 2012. "Myth and Education." In *The Gist: A Celebration of the Imagination* Clarke, edited by Lindsay. UK: The Write Factor.

Hyman, R. 1989. "The Psychology of Deception." *Annual Review of Psychology* 40: 133–154.

Ings, Welby. 2011. "An Assortment of Small Anomalies." in *Inspiring Academics: Learning with the World's Great University Teachers*, edited by Iain Hay. Milton Keynes, UK: Open University Press.

Jackson, Michael. 2002. *The Politics of Storytelling: Violence, Transgression and Intersubjectivity*. Copenhagen: Museum Tusculanum Press.

Jha, A. 2005. "Bursting the Magic Bubble." *The Guardian* (July 28).

Jha, A. 2012. "Young Blood Can Reverse Some Effects of Ageing, Study Finds." *The Guardian* (October 17). http://www.guardian.co.uk/science/2012/oct/17/young-blood-reverse-effects-ageing Website (Accessed October 17, 2012).

Jossey-Bass Publishers. 2003. *The Jossey-Bass Reader on Teaching*. San Francisco: Wiley.

Judt, Tony. 2010. "Night." *The New York Review of Books* (January 14).

Kapuściński, Ryszard. 2008. *The Other*. London: Verso.

Katz, Stephen, and Kevin McHugh. 2010. "Age, Meaning and Place." In *A Guide to Humanistic Studies in Aging: What Does It Mean to Grow Old?* edited by Thomas R. Cole, Ruth Ray, and Robert Kastenbaum, 271–292. Baltimore, MD: The Johns Hopkins University Press.

Kawamoto, W. 2009. "Interview with Arthur Trace: The creative process." About. com: Magic and Illusion. http://magic.about.com/od/biosonfamousmagicians/a/arthurtraceqa.htm (Accessed May 1, 2009).

Keillor, Garrison. 2008. "Wow! America is cool!" (Nov 12) http://www.salon.com/opinion/keillor/2008/11/12/obama_victory/index.html

Kermode. 2006. "Going Against." *London Review of Books* 28(19): 7–8.

Kermode. 2007. "Not Just Yet." *London Review of Books* 29(24):17–18.

King, Martin Luther Jr. 1968. "I've been to the Mountaintop." http://www.afscme.org/union/history/mlk/ive-been-to-the-mountaintop-by-dr-martin-luther-king-jr

Kkoane, Milton Molebatsi, and Jennifer Lavia. 2012. "Rethinking Education in South Africa: Amplifying Liberation Pedagogy." In, *Culture, Education, and Community: Expressions of the Postcolonial Imagination*, edited by Jennifer Lavia and Sechaba Mahlomaholo. New York: Palgrave.

Kloppenberg, James T. 2011. *Reading Obama: Dreams, Hope, and the American Political Tradition*. Princeton, NJ: Princeton University Press.

Kohlberg, Lawrence. 1981. *The Philosophy of Moral Development*. San Francisco: Harper & Row.

Kohlberg, Lawrence. 1984. *The Psychology of Moral Development*. San Francisco Harper & Row.

Kuhn, G. 2009. Home page http://www.dur.ac.uk/gustav.kuhn/Media/Examples.htm (Accessed May 1, 2009).

Kuhn, G., A. Amlani, and R. Rensink. 2008. Towards a science of magic. *Trends in Cognitive Science* 12(9): 349–354.

Kureishi, Hanif. 2006. Amazon Product Description *On Late Style: Music and Literature Against the Grain*.

Kurtz, Howard. 2012. "Democratic Convention Dilemma: Obama 2012 vs. Obama 2008." *The Daily Beast* (September 4).

Lachapelle, S. 2008. "From the Stage to the Laboratory: Magicians, Psychologists, and the Science of Illusion." *Journal of the History of the Behavioural Sciences* 44(4): 319–334.

Lamont, Peter. 2004a. *The Rise of the Indian Rope Trick: The Biography of a Legend*. Boston: Little Brown.

Lamont, Peter. 2004b. The Rediff Interview (August 17-19). http://www.rediff.com/news/2004/aug/19inter.htm (Accessed May 1, 2009).

Lamont, P., and R. Wiseman. 1999. *Magic in Theory: An Introduction to the Theoretical and Psychological Elements of Conjuring*. Hatfield, UK: University of Hertfordshire Press.

Landy, Joshua, and Michael Saler, 2009. "Introduction: The Varies of Modern Enchantment." In *The Re-enchantment of the World: Secular Magic in a Rational Age*, edited by Joshua Landy and Michael Saler. Stanford, CA: Stanford University Press.

Landy, Joshua, and Michael Saler, eds. 2009. *The Re-enchantment of the World: Secular Magic in a Rational Age* Stanford, CA: Stanford University Press.

Larkin, Philip. "The Old Fools." *The Complete Poems of Philip Larkin*.

Lavia, Jennifer and Sechaba Mahlomaholo, eds. 2012. *Culture, Education, and Community: Expressions of the Postcolonial Imagination*. New York: Palgrave.

Lefebvre, Henri. 1947. *Critique of Everyday Life*. Paris: Grasset.

Levinas, Emmanuel. 1972/2003. *Humanism of the Other*. Chicago: University of Illinois Press.

Loeffler, T.A. 2011. "I Teach as the Mountains Teach Me." In *Inspiring Academics: Learning with the World's Great University Teachers*, edited by Iain Hay. Milton Keynes, UK: Open University Press.

Lucas, Ursula. 2011. "Exploring the 'Inner' and 'Outer' Worlds: Steps along a Scholarly Journey." In *Inspiring Academics: Learning with the World's Great University Teachers*, edited by Iain Hay. Milton Keynes, UK: Open University Press.

Maraniss, David. 2012. *Barack Obama: The Story* New York: Simon and Schuster.

Marquez, Gabriel Garcia. 1988. *Love in the Time of Cholera*. Harmondsworth, UK: Penguin.

Marqusee, Mike. 2012. "Let's Talk Utopia." In *Utopia*, edited by Ross Bradshaw. London: Five Leaves Publications.

May, William. 1985. "The Virtues and Vices of the Elderly." In *What Does It Mean to Grow Old?* edited by Thomas Cole and Sally Gadow, 43–61. *Reflections from the Humanities.* Durham, NC: Duke University Press.

McCrum, Robert. 2009. "When Obama Tells a Story, We Listen." *The Observer* (January 25).

McPherson, James M. 2012. "A Bombshell on the American Public." *New York Review of Books* LIX(18): 17–20.

Mieder, Wolfgang. 2009. *"Yes We Can": Barack Obama's Proverbial Rhetoric* New York: Peter Lang.

Miller, Char Roone. 2005. "Neither Palace Nor Temple Nor Tomb: The Lincoln Memorial in the Age of Commercial Reappropriation." In *National symbols, fractured identities: Contesting the national narrative*, edited by Michael Geisler. Middlebury: Middlebury College Press.

Miller, Michelle. 2009. "United by Inspiration." In *Art for Obama: Designing Manifest Hope and the Campaign for Change*, edited by Shepard Fairey and Jennifer Gross. New York: Abrams.

Moat, John. 2012a. "Unfinished Business." In *The Gist: A Celebration of the Imagination*, edited by Lindsay Clarke. UK: The Write Factor.

Moat, John. 2012b. "The Gist of Arvon." In *The Gist: A Celebration of the Imagination*, edited by Lindsay Clarke. UK: The Write Factor.

Modell, Arnold.. 2003. *Imagination and the Meaningful Brain.* Cambridge, MA: MIT Press.

Moody, Harry R. 1992. "Gerontology and Critical Theory." *The Gerontologist* 3, 294–295.

Murphy, Peter "Discovery" in Murphy, Peter, Michael Peter, Simon Marginson. 2010. *Imagination: Three Models of Imagination in the Age of the Knowledge Economy.* Oxford: Peter Lang.

Murphy, Peter, Michael Peter, Simon Marginson. 2010. *Imagination: Three Models of Imagination in the Age of the Knowledge Economy.* Oxford: Peter Lang.

Murray, Penelope. 1991. "Introduction." In *Imagination: A Study in the History of Ideas*, edited by J. M. Cocking. London: Routledge.

Ndlovu, Siyanda. 2008. "The Story of One Black Man" Graduate Guest Seminar Presentation, University of KwaZulu-Natal.

Ndlovu, Siyanda. 2013. Portfolio of Doctoral Work Submitted to the University of KwaZulu-Natal November 2012. Degree awarded 2013.

*New York Times.*1997. "Jeanne Calment, World's Elder, Dies at 122." (August 5). http://www.nytimes.com/1997/08/05/world/jeanne-calment-world-s-elder-dies-at-122.html (Accessed October 24, 2010).

New York Times. 2010. "Robert Butler, Aging Expert, Is Dead at 83." (July 7) http://www.nytimes.com/2010/07/07/health/research/07butler.html (Accessed October 24, 2012).

Nichols, Shaun, ed.. 2006. *The Architecture of the Imagination: New Essays on Pretence, Possibility, and Fiction.* Oxford: Clarendon Press.

Nuland, Sherwin. 1993. *How We Die: Reflections of Life's Final Chapter*, new ed. Vintage Books.

Nussbaum, M. 1997. *Cultivating Humanity.* Cambridge, MA: Harvard University Press.

Nussbaum, Martha. 2001. *The Fragility of Goodness: Luck and Ethics in Greek Tragedy and Philosophy.* Cambridge, UK: Cambridge University Press—or "The Fragility of Goodness" video link http://www.pangeaprogress.com/1/post/2010/08/the-fragility-of-goodness-martha-nussbaum.html

Nussbaum, Martha. 2002. "Education for Citizenship in an Era of Global Connection." *Studies in Philosophy and Education* 21: 289–303.

Nussbaum, Martha. 2010a. *Not for Profit: Why Democracy Needs the Humanities.* Princeton: Princeton University Press.

Nussbaum, Martha. 2010b. 'The fragility of goodness' http://www.pangeaprogress.com/1/post/2010/08/the-fragility-of-goodness-martha-nussbaum.html (Accessed December 11, 2012).

Obama, Barack. 2004. "2004 Democratic National Convention Keynote Address." (July 27). http://www.americanrhetoric.com/speeches/convention2004/barackobama2004dnc (Accessed March 8, 2009).

Obama, Barack. 2005. "What I See in Lincoln's Eyes." *Time* (June 26). http://www.time.com

Obama, Barack. 2006. Emily's List Annual Lunch, Washington, DC (May 11). http://www.guardian.co.uk/world/2009/jan/20/barack-obama-inauguration-speeches-1

Obama, Barack. 2009. "What the People Need Done." Abraham Lincoln Bicentennial (February 12). http://www.scribd.com/doc/12415216/Obama-Speech-at-Lincoln-Association-Banquet-Springfield-IL-21209Obama

Obama, Barack. 2013. Inaugural Address. *The Washington Post* (January 21).

Orgad, Shani. 2012. *Media Representation and the Global Imagination.* Cambridge: Polity.

Palmer, J.-I. 2004. "Review of Jim Steinmeyer's Hiding the Elephant." http://www.nth-position.com/hidingtheelephant.php (Accessed May 1, 2009).

Palmer, Parker. 2003. "The Heart of a Teacher: Identity and Integrity in Teaching." In *The Jossey-Bass Reader on Teaching.* San Francisco: Jossey Bass.

Palmer, Parker. 2007. *The Courage to Teach*, 2nd ed. San Francisco: Wiley.

Pink, S. 2012. *Situating Everyday Life: Practices and Places.* London: Sage.

Polletta, Francesca. 2006. *It Was Like a Fever: Storytelling in Protest and Politics.* Chicago: University of Chicago Press.

Project Vote. 2008. "Minority Voting Surged in 2008 Election, According to Project Vote analysis." (November 25). http://projectvote.org/indexhttp://projectvote.org/index.php?id=80&tx_ttnews%5Btt_news%5D=2726&tx_ttnews%5BbackPid%5D=75&cHash=1fc560e9c7

Proud, Linda. 2012. "The Sweet Voice of Reason." In *The Gist: A Celebration of the Imagination*, edited by Lindsay Clarke. UK: The Write Factor.

Raban, Jonathan. 2009. "The Golden Trumpet." *The Guardian* (January 24). http://www.guardian.co.uk/world/2009/jan/24/barack-obama-inauguration-speech-presidency-president-review-jonathan-raban

Randall, W.L. 2013. "The importance of being ironic. Narrative openness and personal resilience in later life" *Gerontologist* 53(1): 9–16.

Reay, Diane. 2004. "Finding or Losing Yourself? Working-class relationships to education." In *The RoutledgeFalmer Reader in Sociology of Education*, edited by Stephen Ball. London: RoutledgeFalmer.

Regan, Kathleen. 2011. "Seeing the Tree in the Midst of the Forest: Respecting and Supporting the Development of Students as Individuals." In *Inspiring Academics: Learning with the World's Great University Teachers*, edited by Iain Hay. Milton Keynes, UK: Open University Press.

Remarks by the First Lady and the President at Final Campaign Rally—Des Moines, IA." November 6, 2012. http://www.whitehouse.gov/the-press-office/2012/11/06/remarks-first-lady-and-president-final-campaign-rally-des-moines-ia.

Remnick, David. 2010. *The Bridge: The Life and rise of Barack Obama.* New York: Knopf.

Rich, Frank. 2010. "Why Has He Fallen Short?" *New York Review of Books* (August 19).

Ricoeur, Paul. 1984. *Time and Narrative*. Chicago: University of Chicago Press.

Ricoeur, Paul. 2004. *Memory, History, Forgetting*. Chicago: University of Chicago Press.

Riley, Denise. 2012. *Time Lived Without Its Flow*. London: Capsule Editions.

Riessman, C. 2008. *Narrative Methods for the Human Sciences*. London: Sage.

Riessman, Catherine Kohler. 2008. *Narrative Methods for the Human Sciences*. London: Sage.

Rutenberg, Jim. 2012. "Raising G.O.P., Ryan Faults 'Missing' Leadership." *The New York Times* (August 29).

Said, Edward. 2004. "Thoughts on Late Style." *London Review of Books* 26(15): 3–7

Said, Edward. 2007. *On Late Style: Music and Literature Against the Grain*. London: Bloomsbury.

Sail, Lawrence. 2012. "Sixteens." *The Gist: A Celebration of the Imagination*, edited by L. Clarke. UK: The Write Factor.

Salmon, Philida and Catherine Riessman. 2008. "Looking Back on Narrative Research: An Exchange." In *Doing Narrative Research*, edited by M. Andrews, C. Squire, and M. Tamboukou. London: Sage.

Sartre, J. P. 1940/1972. *The Psychology of Imagination*. London: Methuen.

Schama, Simon. 2009. "The Great Hope." *The Independent* (January 24). http://www.independent.co.uk/news/presidents/simon-schama-the-great-hope--barack-obama-1482927.html

Scherer, Michael. 2012. "2012 Person of the Year: Barack Obama, the President." *Time* (December 19). http://poy.time.com/2012/12/19/person-of-the-year-barack-obama (Accessed April 1, 2013).

Schwartz, Barry. 1990. "The Reconstruction of Abraham Lincoln." In *Collective Remembering*, edited by David Middleton and Derek Edwards. London: Sage.

Schwartz, Barry. 2000. *Abraham Lincoln and the Forge of National Memory*. Chicago: University of Chicago Press.

Scott, S. 2009. *Making Sense of Everyday Life* Cambridge, UK: Polity.

Selbin, Eric. 2011. *Revolution, Rebellion, Resistance: The Power of Story*. London: Zed Books.

Shankardass, Mala Kapur. 2010. "Aging with Dignity." *The Hindu* (August 7).

Sherringham, M. 2009. *Everyday Life: Theories and Practices from Surrealism to the Present* Oxford, UK: Oxford University Press.

Sikes, P. 1997. *Parents Who Teach: Stories From Home and From School*. London: Cassells.

Solnit, Rebecca. 2005. *A Field Guide to Getting Lost*. New York: Viking.

Steinmeyer, J. 1998. *Art and Artifice and Other Essays on Illusion*. New York: Carroll and Graf.

Stengel, Richard, Michael Scherer, and Radhika Jones. 2012. "Setting the Stage for a Second Term." *Time* (December 19). http://poy.time.com/2012/12/19/setting-the-stage-for-a-second-term/ (Accessed April 1, 2013).

Stevenson, Richard. 2013. "A Call for Progressive Values: Evolved, Unapologetic and Urgent." *The New York Times* (January 22), A11.

Stoetzler, M. and N. Yuval-Davis. 2002. "Standpoint Theory, Situated Knowledge—and the Situated Imagination." *Feminist Theory* 3(3):315–334.

Sugrue, Thomas J. 2010. *Not Even Past: Barack Obama and the Burden of Race*. Princeton, NJ: Princeton University Press.

Sundaram, Chitra. 2007. "Love and Authenticity in the Age of Anxiety—Dance and Ageing." *Animated: The Community Dance Magazine*: 11. http://www.communitydance.org.uk/DB/animated-library/love-and-authenticity-in-the-age-of-anxiety-dance-.html?ed=14048 (Accessed 2 September 2013).

Taper, Jake. 2008. "Michelle Obama: 'For the first time in my adult lifetime, I'm really proud of my country.'" *ABC News Political Punch* (February 18). http://blogs.abcnews.com/politicalpunch/2008/02

Terkel, Studs. 1995. *Coming of Age: The Story of our Century by Those Who've Lived It*. New York: St. Martin's Griffin.

Thomson, David. 2012. "Spielberg's *Lincoln* Is a Film for Our Political Moment." *The New Yorker* (November 13). http://www.tnr.com/article/books-and-arts/110113/spielbergs-lincoln-film-our-political-moment#

Thomas, W.I. and D.S. Thomas. 1928. *The Child in America: Behavior Problems and Programs*. New York: Knopf.

Tilly, Charles. 2002. *Stories, Identities and Political Change*. New York: Rowman & Littlefield.

Torre, Maria Elena and Michelle Fine. 2008. "Participatory Action Research in the Contact Zone." In *Revolutionizing Education: Youth Participatory Action Research in Motion*, edited by Julio Cammarota and Michelle Fine. London: Routledge.

Travers, K. 2009 "Obama Celebrates Lincoln's Bicentennial with 'Special Gratitude'." *Political Punch* (February 12). http://blogs.abcnews.com/political-punch/2009/02/obama-celebrate.html

Ulaby, Neda. 2008. "Toni Morrison on Bondage and a Post-Racial Age." *Tell Me More*. NPR (December 10). http://www.npr.org/templates/story/story.php?storyId=98072491

von Wright, Moira. 2002. "Narrative Imagination and Taking the Perspective of Others." *Studies in Philosophy and Education* 21(4–5): 407–416.

Wallace, Milverton. 2008. "Brits Seems [sic] to Love (and Read Books of] the next U.S. President." http://www.brooklynron.com/dreams-from-my-father/

Walters, Joanna. 2008. "'Little Rock Nine' prepare to celebrate day of victory." *The Observer* (December 28). http://www.guardian.co.uk/world/2008/dec

Warnock, Mary. 1940/1972. "Introduction" to Jean Paul Sartre *The Psychology of Imagination*. London: Methuen.

Warnock, Mary. 1976. *Imagination*. London: Faber and Faber.

Warnock, Mary. 1989. *Universities: Knowing Our Minds*. London: Chatto & Windus.

Warnock, Mary. 1994. *Imagination and Time*. Oxford, UK: Blackwell.

Warnock, Mary. 2011. Personal interview (March 7).

Williams, Raymond. 1988. *Resources of Hope: Culture, Democracy, Socialism*. London: Verso.

Wiseman, R. 2007. *Quirkology: The Curious Science of Everyday Lives*. London: Macmillan.

Wood, Michael. 2006. "Introduction." In *On Late Style: Music and Literature Against the Grain*, edited by Edward Said. London: Bloomsbury.

Wurtele, Susan. 2011. "Beyond the Classroom Walls: Using Assessment Strategies to Foster Independent learning." In *Inspiring Academics: Learning with the World's Great University Teachers*, edited by Iain Hay. Milton Keynes, UK: Open University Press.

Wyatt-Brown, Anne. 2010. "Resilience and Creativity in Aging: The Realms of Silver." In *A Guide to Humanistic Studies in Aging: What Does It Mean to Grow Old?* edited by Thomas R. Cole, Ruth Ray, and Robert Kastenbaum, 57–82. Baltimore, MD: The Johns Hopkins University Press.

Yuval-Davis, Nira. 2011. *The Politics of Belonging: Intersectional Contestations*. London: Sage.

Zeleny, Jeff. 2008. "On Eve of Election, Obama Pays Tribute to Grandmother Who Died in Hawaii." *The New York Times* (November 3). http://www.nytimes.com/2008/11/04

Zingaro, Linde. 2009. *Speaking Out: Storytelling for Social Change*. Walnut Creek, CA: Left Coast.

CREDIT LINES

INDEX